SPEAK DUTCH BUNDLE

3 IN 1

Speak Dutch

Book 1 of 3: Beginners

By Vincent Noot

Copyright @2015

All rights reserved. No part of this book may be reproduced in any form or by any means without permission in writing from the publisher, Vincent Noot.

If you like my book, please leave a positive review on Amazon. I would appreciate it a lot. Thanks! This is the link:

Subscribe to my blog: lifechangingebooksblog.blogspot.com

You can also visit my Facebook page.

Or you can look at my Pinterest board.

Contents:

Introduction   4

Chapter 1: Pronunciation   7

Chapter 2: Easy Words   20

Chapter 3: Small Words   31

Chapter 4: Numbers   39

Chapter 5: Animals   48

Chapter 6: Body Parts   73

Chapter 7: Food   76

Chapter 8: Family   81

Chapter 9: Verbs, Present Tense   84

Chapter 10: Simple Phrases and Conjunctions   92

Introduction

This book is for beginners, people who haven't learned any Dutch at all, but are excited to get started.

As you might have seen from my last name (and yes, that's my actual name), I am of Dutch origin. In fact, I grew up in the Netherlands. My native language is Dutch, but over the years, as I have lived in several English speaking countries and interacted with many foreigners, I have mastered that language as well. I now speak both languages fluently to the point where most people can't even hear my Dutch accent anymore.

In the past, I have worked for a translation office (English to Dutch), and have become precise and exact at translating, correcting, reviewing, and proofing documents in both Dutch and English. Because of my experience in translation work and numerous editing jobs, and with my cultural background, I am confident to say that I will be one of the best Dutch language teachers you'll find. I will show you how to learn and master the Dutch language in a heartbeat.

Languages are elaborate; they include hundreds of thousands of words (just check out the dictionary) and expressions people "just get used to" when they grow up with a certain language. But memorizing a dictionary will, however useful, only get you so far. Forming sentences and understanding grammar, the logic, and structure of a language is a whole study. One can only speak a language fluently by being completely imbedded in it for years. But at least with these 3 books, I can teach you the most important basics, and get you going, so that you'll be more confident in speaking up and reading or writing Dutch.

The ebook version of this book contains several YouTube video BONUS links to help you with the pronunciation. Check them out!

One of the BEST ways to learn a language, is by learning the most common verbs. Verbs like *to be, to have, to see, to ask, to say, to go, to come, to get*, etc. form the basis of any sentence. I will get you started on the present tense in this book, as well as a lot of other useful topics. Are you eager to learn? Then don't wait any longer and read on. "Ik zie je zo" (I will see you soon).

Chapter 1: Pronunciation

Before we study anything else, you'll have to know how to pronounce the language. I remember a funny experience I had when I was working at an American call center. It was a disaster, because when people spelled their name, the sounds of the alphabet didn't click in my mind quickly enough. So when a New Yorker with a heavy accent said "a," my mind thought it was an "e" and when she said "e," it took me a few seconds to realize it was actually not an "i."

If you don't, whatever you say will be off and misunderstood. So, without further ado, let's start out with the basics. In these books, I will try to relate English words that are said in a similar way to the Dutch pronunciation, and I will include some links to YouTube videos, so you can check what I mean. First, let me point out some pronunciation rules.

En... en als je dan de wereld hebt veroverd? Wat ga je dan doen? (En... en uls yŭ done dŭ we-rŭlt hept fair-oa-vŭrt? Wut ĝah yŭ done doon?) - And... and when you have conquered the world? What are you going to do then?

Nou... uh... (Now... uh...) - Well... errr....

Short Vowels

Just remember that English has a lot of long vowels. Words like "awe," "jaw," "well," "bore," "creek," and almost everything else is pronounced as if they drag the tone all the way to the other side of the world. Not in Dutch however. In Dutch, a lot of vowels are short. Keep that in mind when you try to pronounce the words. If you know German, Spanish, Portuguese, or French, it's good to compare those a little. In those languages, a lot of vowels are short too, just like in Dutch, and the way they pronounce the alphabet is closer to how the Dutch pronounce it.

No "th"

First and foremost, the Dutch do NOT have a "th" sound like the English language does. Words like "the," "thing," "faith" and others are non-existent in the Dutch language. If you ever encounter a word with the "th" in it, simply pronounce the "t" and don't worry about the "h" after it. Often these words come from the ancient Greek language, which is why they are spelled with an "h." Examples are,

theoloog (pronounced: tay-o-logue) - theologists

thee (pronounced: tay) - tea

theorie (pronounced: tay-o-ree) - theory

The "g" or "ch"

The "g" - sound, sometimes written as "ch," which also sometimes comes from Greek, like the word "chaos," is pronounced as a back throat sound, similar to the Spanish "j." It's kind of like gurgling. You may think this sounds terrible, but it can actually sound pretty, depending on where you go and what voice utters the sound. In the Netherlands and Belgium, the way it is, is usually that the further you go north, the louder and harder this letter is pronounced. In the southern Belgian parts, when I lived there, it was almost close to an "h" sometimes and was pronounced softly. In the pronunciation, I will indicate this sound with a "ĝ." Examples are:

chaos (ĝaw-os) - chaos

groen (ĝroon) - green

geven (ĝayvun) - to give

gek (ĝeck) - crazy

kachel (kawĝol) - heater

The "r"

The letter "r" can be pronounced as an English "r," but usually only at the end of a word, which is what they often do in cities like Den Haag (The Hague) or Zoetermeer. In other parts in the Netherlands, it is done occasionally, but often, there is more preference for the French "r." Pronounce it as with the back of your throat. Sometimes it can be so close to the Dutch "ĝ" sound that it's hard to hear the difference. Examples:

rood (roat) - red

ver (fair) - far

heer (here) - gentleman

teer (tere) - tar

A Lot of "u" Sounds

No, not the "u" as in "you," but kind of like the "u" in "urgent," or like the "i" in "birth." Dutch has this sound so much that you better get used to it. So from now on, I will indicate this sound in the pronunciation as "ŭ" so you know that this is what I mean.

The Confusing Letter "e"

The letter "e" can be pronounced, in general, in 3 different ways in Dutch:

1) as in the first "e" in "letter" or "better" or as in "bet" or "bed."

2) as in the "u" sound I just described and I will indicate so by writing it as "ŭ".

3) as "ay" like "bay" or "hay" or "say" or "bait."

This makes it a little complicated, since some words have two or even three different "e"-s in it, but they are pronounced differently. The same counts for English anyway, so maybe it's fair, right? Here are some examples. Look closely at the pronunciation.

veters (vay-tŭrs) - shoe laces

gebrek (ĝŭ-breck) - deficiency

lekken (leck-kŭn) - leaks

gegeten (ĝŭ-ĝay-tŭn) - eaten

verder (fair-dŭr) - farther/further

kever (kay-vŭr) - beetle

Don't Blow

There are three letters in Dutch that are the same, except for the fact that they don't blow the sounds. Those are: P, K, T. For example, you can say the word "parrot" and blow the "p" and "t" as if there was an "h" or something that made you blow the sound. In Dutch, however, they keep them short and cut them off in their pronunciation. The same goes for words with the letter "k" or "c" pronounced as "k." Try pronouncing the following words without blowing those three letters.

beker (bay-kŭr) - cup

takken (taw-kŭn) - branches

ketting (ket-ting) - chain

kapot (kaw-pote) - broken

boeken (boo-kŭn) - books

kaak (kawk) - jaw

kast (kawst) - closet

papegaai (paw-pŭĝ-i) - parrot

teen (tain) - toe

kraan (crawn) - faucet/tap

The "w," an Inbetweeny

The Dutch pronounce the "w" as a letter that is in between a "v" and an English "w." When an English speaking person pronounces the "w," he or she shapes the mouth in a round shape and uses more of his or her front lips to pronounce the letter. The Dutch, however, almost make it sound like a "v," but if you listen closely, it is not the same. Look at the YouTube video to find out how.

Click HERE for the YouTube video.

Slack Off

If you pronounce the letter "z" and the letter "v" exactly like they are, you could get away with it easily and sound good at Dutch, but in a lot of areas in the Netherlands and some in Belgium, for example, people turn the "v" into an "f" and the "z" into an "s." My name, for example, sounded more like "Fincent" than "Vincent." Try pronouncing these words by turning the "v" into an "f"-sound and the "z" into an "s"-sound. It will make it sound more Dutch, I promise.

zelden (sel-dŭn) - seldom/rarely

zaden (saw-dŭn) - seeds

vorig (fow-riĝ) - previous

vaak (fawk) - often

Other things a lot of Dutch leave out, as opposed to the Germans, is the end letter "n." A lot of verbs or plural words end at "-en," but the Dutch don't want to pronounce the "n." Often, the "e" before the last latter has the "ŭ"- sound, so that this common sound get ended with. Sometimes they DO pronounce it if the next word starts with a vowel, just to connect the flow of the words better. It's not incorrect to pronounce the "n," just like in the previous examples, but it makes it sound more Dutch to leave it out sometimes, and by reading this information, you will know what they mean when they leave that letter out. Here are some examples:

geven (ĝay-fŭ) - to give

lopen (low-pŭ) - to walk

taken (taw-kŭ) - tasks

papieren (paw-pee-rŭ) - papers

Watch out that you only leave the "n" out, or can expect them to, when the last two letters are "-en." For example, you could NOT leave it out when you say "doen," "gaan" or "van."

The Letter "D" at the End of a Word

As opposed to the English, the Dutch don't like to end with a "d" sound. In English it's common to make sure you perfect your pronunciation by indicating that a word ends with a "d" in words like "end," "bend," "hand," "fond," etc. In Dutch, this letter turns into a "t." So someone with a heave Dutch accent may pronounce those words like "ent," "bent," "hant," "font," etc. Practice these words and turn the "d" at the end of the word into a "t."

hard (heart) - hard

paard (pahrt) - horse

gerend (ĝŭ-rent) - ran

rond (rohnt) - round

moord (moart) - murder

The Alphabet

Okay, with all these tricks and techniques, you are now ready for the offical alphabet

A - awe (but open up your mouth further)

B - bay

C - say

D - day

E - aye

F - ef

G - ĝay

H - haw (but open up your mouth further)

I - ee

J - yay

K - kaw (but open up your mouth further)

L - el

M - em

N - en

O - owe

P - pay

Q - queue

R - air

S - es

T - tay

U - you (without the "y")

V - vay

W - way

X - ix

Y - I (similar to the word "I")

Z - zet

Vowel Combinations

Just like in English certain combinations or vowels create different sounds, the Dutch have some set combinations of vowels. However, it might be hard for an English speaking person to get all of them exactly right, since some of them don't exist in English. If you bought an E-book version of this book, you could click on the link to the YouTube video.

[Click HERE for the YouTube video.](#)

au - ou (as in "cow" or "now")

Examples: kauwen, nauw, authentiek

ou - ou (as in "cow" or "now," whether the Dutch spelling is with the first "au" or the second "au" depends on the word. There is no way to tell by the sound.)

Examples: oud, hout, rouwen, mouw, vrouw

eu - ew (not exactly the same sound, but if you want to get it right, go to the YouTube video above

Examples: heus, keuze, leuk, reus, peuk, deuken

ui - sounds a little like "ou" but is still different (listen to the YouTube video to hear the difference through the link above)

Examples: huis, kuis, muis, ruit, buiten, fluiten

ei - similar to the word "I" (hear the difference in the video)

Examples: meisje, Eiffeltoren, eikels, zeiden, dreigen

ij - exactly the same pronunciation as the Dutch "ei"-combination

Examples: ijsje, vrij, krijgen, strijden, hij, zij, wij, blijven

ie - "ee" but less exaggerated and shorter, like in "to be," "free," and "flee"

Examples: fiets, kiezen, liep, riep, hier, mieren, brie

oe - like in "shoe" but shorter

Examples: koe, stoer, boer, hoed, meerkoet, hoes

Besides these standard vowel combinations, it makes a difference whether the Dutch write a word with one or two vowels. Make sure you get these right, because if you don't, you might be saying a different word. When I lived in the

Netherlands, I knew an American visitor who tried to say, "We gaan naar het bos" (We are going to the forest). But instead he said, "We gaan naar het boos" (We are going to the angry). Luckily, we knew what he meant, but it just shows that one or two vowels can make all the difference.

Usually, one vowel means a short sound, and two of the same vowels in a row means a long sound. Study the following single or double vowel combinations in order to understand the difference in pronunciation.

a - short, so kind of like in "duck" or "buck" or "suck."

Examples: dak, slak, takken, stakker, kapot, hakken

aa - long, so a little like "awe" or "raw" or "jaw" but open your mouth further and pronounce it like a Spanish "a"

Examples: taart, kaart, haat, staak, maak, maan

u - usually like the "ŭ"- sound I pointed out earlier, like in "fur" or "stir" or "heard"

Examples: hut, durven, huppelen, ruk, stuk, put

uu - like in "ew" but without the "w," like in "new" or "dew" or "crew"

Examples: muur, duur, stuur, huur, infuus, vuur

Funny side note: I knew someone who mistakenly said she was going to pay the "hoer" (whore) that month instead of the "huur" (rent - think of "hire"). We laughed pretty hard.

o - short, so like in "bore" or "store" or "more"

Examples: bos, stop, kop, rotten, lok, krop, dom

oo - long, so like in "boat" or "road" or "yoke" or "coat." Don't forget that it's not an English "oo" or "ew" sound like in "boot" or "foot." This is why so many people in English speaking countries pronounce my name "Noot" wrong. It should be pronounced as "note."

Examples: noot, rood, groot, rook, loop

By the way, when the double "oo" is followed by an "r," it usually sounds like the short "o," like in "before" or "chore."

Examples: voor, oor, oord, koord, woord

e - pretty simple, like in "bell" or "tell" or "leapt" or "neck."

Examples: nek, vet, het, red, lek, mep

ee - sound like "ay" in English, such as in "stay" or "clay" or "stake" or "mate" or "claim."

Examples: meet, steek, reeks, beek, leek, vrees

By the way, when the double "ee" combination is followed by an "r," it sound more like an "i" or "ere" or "ear."

Examples: meer, teer, heer, leer, keer

i - this letter is pronounced as the sound "fit" or "kit" or "whit."

Examples: hik, dik, fit, kin, vin, mis

Sometimes, it is pronounced as an "ee" like in "glee" or "steep" or "feature." This is never the case if it concerns a word with only one syllable.

Examples: direct, miserabel, idioot, virus, crimineel

Just for spelling purposes, it's useful to know that the Dutch sometimes use what they call, a "trema," two dots on a vowel to indicate that the syllable changes in the middle of that word. It is just for pronunciation purposes and means nothing else. You don't have to memorize this, but it is just good to know about it. Here are some examples.

egoïsme
coördinatie
ruïne,
vacuüm
naïviteit
reële
geïnd
reünie
conciërge
koloniën
poëzie

Chapter 2: Easy Words

You can find words in many languages that sound, look, or feel like a word in English or some other language you already know. You can do this with any language, but with Dutch, it can be particularly easy, since Dutch, German, and English are considered to be Germanic languages. Therefore, sometimes all that changes, is a vowel or two and the pronunciation, but the meaning and the consonants remain almost the same. Check out the list below. It may seem like a lot of words to memorize, but it's actually really easy. I bet you'll have them down by going over them twice or sometimes even once.

Almost or Exactly the Same

bar (pronounced the same) - bar

noedels (pronounced the same, but short vowels) - noodles

legende (lŭĝendŭ) - legend

sok (sork, without the "r") - sock

neus (almost like "news") - nose

hoed (hoot) - hat

gras (ĝraws) - grass

plant (plont) - plant

grond (ĝront) - ground

peper (pay-pŭr) - pepper

envelop (en-vŭ-lop) - envelope

boot (boat) - boat

peer (peer) - pear

bus (bŭs) - bus

staren (stah-rŭn) - to stare

pizza (same word) - pizza

poker (poker) - poker

ketchup (ketchŭp) - ketchup

lasagna (lasagna) - lasagna

vakantie (faw-kŭn-see) - vacation

letter (same pronunciation, make sure you say the "t") - letter

pen ("pen" but don't blow the "p") - pen

lood (lowt) - lead

wit (whit) - white

mat (mut) - mat

tafel (taw-fŭl) - table

soep ("soup" with a short vowel) - soup

deur (dewr) - door

wagen (wah-ĝŭn) - wagon

kussen (kŭssŭn) - pillow (think of "cushion")

bed (bet) - bed

televisie (taylayveesee) - television

tv (tayvay) - TV

computer (pronounced the same, except the "e" = ŭ) - computer duivel (dowvel) - devil

God (ĝot) - God

engel (engŭl) - angel

vork (fork) - fork

auto (auto) - car (think of "automobile")

telefoon (taylŭphone) - telephone

trompet (trompet, with emphasis on "-pet") - trumpet

hoorn (horn) - French horn

viool (fee-oal) - violin

piano (pee-ano) - piano

drums (drŭms) - drums

kat (cut) - cat

poes (poose) - cat (think of pussycat)

lamp (lump) - lamp

licht (liĝt) - light

sorry (sow-ree) - sorry

bank (bunk) - bank (as in "a bank company with money, not a couch")

huis (house) - house

hand (hunt) - hand

thuis (touse) - home

muis (mouse) - mouse

droom (drome) - dream

rijst (ricet) - rice

spinazie (spee-nah-see) - spinache

bei (by) - bee

bij (pronounced the same as the other "bei") - by

jaloers (yah-loo-rs) - jealous

tofu (tofu) - tofu

hamer (hah-mŭr) - hammer

foto (foto) - photograph

t-shirt (pronounced the same) - T-shirt

koala (pronounced the same) - koala bear

aap (awp) - monkey (think of "ape")

muur (mure) - wall (think of "mural")

beer (bere) - bear (as in "an animal bear")

bier (beer) - beer (the alcoholic drink)

meer (mere) - more

banaan (ba-nahn) - banana

vuur (fure) - fire

stok (stowk) - stick

wiel (pronounced the same, but short vowel) - wheel

draak (drahk) - dragon

goed (ĝoot) - good/well

beter (bay-tŭr) - better

best (pronounced exactly the same) - best

in (pronounced exactly the same) - in

uit (pronounced slightly different) - out/off

kom (comb) - come

ga (ĝah) - go

heb (hep) - have

datum (dah-tŭm) - date

dat (dot) - that

dit (dit) - this

steen (stain) - stone

oor (ore) - ear

zon ("sown" but short vowel) - sun

zoon ("sown" but long vowel) - son

dochter (doĝtŭr) - daughter

kind ("kint" rhymes with "mint") - child/kid

maan (mawn) - moon

navel (nah-vŭl) - navel

cd (sayday) - CD

dvd (dayvayday) - DVD

souvenir (pronounced the same) - souvenir

historisch (hee-store-ees) - historical

student ("stew-dent" with emphasis on "-den") - student

jou (yow) - you (object)

jij ("yay" rhymes with "bye") - you (subject)

we (wŭ) - we

toernooi (tour-noy) - tournament

sport (pronounced the same) - sport

rol (roll/role) - either as in "fulfilling a role" or as in "roll over"

rond (runt) - round

ijs ("ice," but slightly different) - ice or ice cream

water (watŭr, make sure you pronounce the "t" but don't blow it) - water

wind (wint) - wind

appel (aw-pel) - apple

straat (strawt) - street

blok (blohk) - block

eten (ay-ten) - food/to eat

rouw ("row" rhymes with "plow") - raw

rat (rut) - rat

vet ("fet") - fat

dik (dick) - thick/fat

waar (wahr) - where

daar (dahr) - there

pan (pun) - pan

pot (powt) - pot (say the vowel short, or it would be "poot" which means "paw")

zwaard (swahrt) - sword

schild (sĝilt) - shield

helm (helm) - helmet

depressie (day-pres-see) - depression

Latin or Germanic

One of the main differences between English and the other two Germanic languages, Dutch and German, is that English uses a lot more Latin-based words. Sometimes, a word makes a lot of sense in Dutch because it is a combination of other words that have their root in the Germanic origins, but the English deviates from German or Dutch because it uses a word with Latin roots. Here are some interesting examples of words that make sense if you explain them.

aardappel (awrt-opple) - potato

This word consists of 2 words: "aard" and "appel." The word "aard" comes from "aarde" which means "earth" and the word "appel" simply means "apple." Since a potato is a starch that roots in the soil, the word "earth apple" makes a lot of sense, doesn't it?

schildpad (sĝilt-pot) - turtle

The word "schild" means "shield" and the word "pad" means "toad." Therefore, the Dutch call a turtle a "shield toad."

aardbei (ahrt-by) - strawberry

The word "aard" as we saw earlier, means "earth" and the word "bei" is another word for "bes" which means "berry." So strawberries are actually called "earth berries" since they don't grow on trees but on low, little plants.

vierkant (fear-kunt) - square

The word "vier" simply means "four" and the word "kant" means "side." Pretty easy, right? A square is called a "four side" in Dutch, since it has four sides.

driehoek (dree-hook) - triangle

This is one of those words for which the English decided to go the Latin way, but the Dutch kept it simple and called it what it is. The word "drie" means "three" and the word "hoek" means corner. Thus, a triangle is called "three corner" in Dutch.

bloemkool (bloom-cole) - cauliflower

The word "bloem" means "flower" (think of "blooming"), and the word "kool" means "cabbage." Therefore, a cauliflower is called "flower cabbage" in Dutch, and that's what it looks like, doesn't it?

frisdrank (friss-drunk) - soda (pop)

Literally, the word "fris-drank" just means "fresh drink." Makes sense, right? Those this is what you ask for if you want a general idea of their selection of coke, orange soda, lime (7up, Sprite), or, what they often have in the Netherlands: Black currant, which they call "cassis" (it's delicious, try it.)

sinaassappel (see-nah-sup-pŭl) - orange (the fruit; the color is called "oranje" [oh-run-yŭ])

The addition "sinaass" simply refers to the fact that this is a citrus fruit. The word "appel" means "apple." So an orange is called a "citrus apple."

plakband (pluck-bunt) - tape/scotch tape

The word "plak" comes from "plakken" which means to paste, glue, or stick something. The word "band" is like a band (not the musical), like a rubber band.

handdoek (hunt-duke) - towel

The word "hand" means "hand" and "doek" is a rag or cloth. Therefore, a towel is simply called a "hand cloth" in Dutch. Makes sense, doesn't it? Since you often use it to dry your hands after washing them.

verder gaan (fair-dŭr ĝahn) - continue

The word "verder" means "further/farther" and the word "gaan" means "to go." This is one of those cases where the English chose a Latin word and the Dutch integrated a Germanic combination of two words. Another word for it could also be "doorgaan" which means the same ("door" means "through").

vrachtwagen (fruĝt-wah-ĝŭn) - semi truck

The word "vracht" literally means "freight" so a "vrachtwagen" is actually a "freight wagon." That is pretty much what a semi truck is, isn't it?

voorzichtig (four-siĝt-iĝ) - careful/cautious

Literally "voorzichtig" means "fore-sight-ful," or in other words: If you see ahead and you let your sight be a guide before you, you are be cautious or careful.

losmaken (loss-mah-kŭn) - detach, loosen up

The word "los" means "loose" and the word "maken" means "to make." So the Dutch talk about "making your shoe laces loose" instead of "untying your shoe laces." Just a fun side note: Laces are "veters." So you could say, "Maak je veters los" (untie your shoes).

As you've seen in some of these examples, the Dutch use words that are very different from the English meaning, but if you understand the logic behind those words, it will be easier to memorize them.

Underneath are some examples, though, where the Dutch has integrated the Latin root too. Therefore, they are close to English and easy to guess or remember. Take a quick look at these:

concluderen (con-clue-dear-ŭn) - conclude

competitie (com-pŭ-tee-tsee) - competition

compact (com-puckt) - compact

combinatie (com-bee-nah-tsee) - combination

inclusief (in-clue-seaf) - including

recessie (rŭ-ces-see) - recession

natie (nah-tsee) - nation

extra (extra) - extra

extrovert (extrovert) - extrovert

integreren (in-tŭ-ĝrere-ŭn) - integrate

informatie (in-for-mah-tsee) - information

contract (con-truckt) - contract

Chapter 3: Small Words

Now that you have some knowledge and more understanding of the basics of the Dutch language, you'll be able to go on and memorize more easily what's being taught. First, you need to understand how a language makes sense, the logic of their thinking patterns. And only then, the rest falls into place. In this chapter, we'll go over some of the most prevalent, little words you need to remember in order to create simple sentences.

Hoor

The word "hoor" (and yes, it's pronounced as "whore" or "hoar") means something like the old English "hear." When people say this, don't be offended. They are not calling you a whore. They are simply emphasizing what they just said. For example:

Ik ga niet weg. (Ik ĝah neet weĝ.) - I am not going away.

Ik ga niet weg, hoor. (Ik ĝah neet weĝ, hoar.) - I am really not going away. Don't worry.

"The" or "A"

In Dutch, there are two words for "the" and only one word for "a" or "an."

The = de/het

A/an = een

De word "de" is pronounced as "dŭ" or a little like the English expression "duh!" The word "een" is often pronounced as "ŭn." De word "het" is pronounced exactly how it looks.

So how can you know whether you should use "de" or "het"? Well, I hate to tell you this, but most times, you just need to memorize which one it is. It's like the Spanish "el" or "la" or like the French "le" or "la" or the German "der," "die" and "das."

So anytime you learn a noun in Dutch, always try to memorize if it's "de" or "het." It can be completely annoying to find out dat het "de doek" is, but "het boek." And that it is "het gedoe" but "de koe." So just because it rhymes, doesn't mean it has the same gender.

However, I will give you a few tricks that work most times, just so that, if you are guessing, you have a higher chance of being right.

Words that end with "-je" are usually diminished words. More about that in the last book in this series. For now, it's useful to know that they are always "het." So, for example:

het meisje (het mice-yŭ) - the girl

het visje (het fis-yŭ) - the little fish (even though it's "de vis")

het liedje (het lee-tyŭ) - the little song

Plural is ALWAYS "de," even if the singular form is "het." Just remember that. See the following examples for the singular form and the plural right next to it.

het boek - de boeken (books)

het ding - de dingen (things)

het vak - de vakken (subjects)

het vlot - de vloten (rafts)

het gebod - de geboden (commandments)

There are some more rules to determine which it is, but those are a little more complicated. There are more words with "de" than with "het" so if you really doubt and you have to make a guess, just go for "de" since the chance is higher you guessed it right.

This/that/these/those

The words go along with the gender ("de" or "het") and with the singular or plural form. Check them out below:

that = dat (when it concerns "het"), pronounce as *dot*

that = die (when it concerns "de"), pronounce as *dee*

this = dit (if it concerns "het"), pronounce as *dit*

this = deze (if it concerns "de"), pronounce as *day-sŭ*

So, for example, if you want to say "this book" you figure out first that it's "het boek" and therefore, it becomes "dit boek." If you want to say, for example "that train," you look it up and find that it is "de trein." So that means it should be "die trein." Again, if you aren't sure and you have to guess at a certain moment without time to look it up, just go for "die" and "deze," since there is a higher chance you'll guess right.

The plural is easier. With the plural form, it doesn't matter if the word belonging to the noun is "de" or "het." It remains the same, which makes it easier to memorize. See?

those = die, pronounce as *dee*

these = deze, pronounce as *day-sŭ*

Colors

I will show you the most important and commonly used colors, so you can point to stuff and say what color it is, or tell the guy at the store what color paint you want to buy.

Rood (roat) - red

Blauw (blouw) - blue

Wit (whit) - white

Zwart (swart) - black

Geel (ĝale) - yellow

Groen (ĝrewn) - green

Oranje (oh-run-yŭ) - orange

Paars (pawrs) - purple

Rose (roh-sŭ) - pink

Grijs (ĝrice) - grey

Bruin (brown, but not exactly) - brown

Licht (liĝt) - light

Donker (don-kŭr) - dark

Mijn hond heet Bruno, want hij is bruin! (Mine hoant hate Bruno, wunt high is brown!) - My dog's name is Bruno, because he is brown

Die van mij heet Kees! Het is een keeshond! (Mine hoant hate Case! Het is ŭn case-hoant!) - My dog's name is Kees! It is a spitz!"

Onze hond heet Vaatwasser! (Oan-sŭ hoant hate Vaht-wassŭr!) - Our dog's name is Dishwasher!

Maar... waarom dan? (Mahr... wah-roam done?) - But... why then?

Hij likt de borden schoon! (High lickt dŭ boar-dŭn sĝoan!) - He licks the plates clean!

The Dutch combine their words often, so "dark blue" would be "donkerblauw" and "light red" would be "lichtrood."

Greetings

Here are some common greetings in Dutch.

hoi (hoy) - hi

hallo (hollow) - hello

goedendag (ĝoo-dŭn-duhĝ) - good day

dag (duhĝ) - goodbye

tot ziens (toht seens) - goodbye/untiil we meet again

tot later (toht lahter) - see you later

hoe gaat het? (who ĝaht het?) - how are you?

goed (ĝoot) - good

Wel/Niet

In English, as in any other language, there is a difference between "yes" and "no." In Dutch, these expressions are "ja" (yah), which is the same as in German, and "nee" (nay) like the old English word for "no."

However, the word that English is missing, is the opposite of the word "not." When trying to indicate the affirmative, English speakers often use the word "do" or put an extra strong emphasis on the verb in the sentence. For example, someone might say, "You did NOT take out the garbage," to which another may respond, "That's not true. I DID take out the garbage." Obviously the English never made up a word that opposes the word "not," but the Dutch did. Yay!

The Dutch word for "not" is "niet" (neat) and the opposite is "wel" (well). Consider the following expressions, for instance:

Dat is niet mooi (That is not pretty) - Het is wel mooi (It IS pretty).

Niet waar (Not true) - Wel waar (It IS true).

Je mag niet met ons mee (You may not come with us) - Ik mag wel met jullie mee (I MAY come with you).

Ik heb het niet gedaan (I didn't do it) - Je hebt het wel gedaan (Je DID do it).

Even

The word "even" (pronounced as "ay-fŭ") is often used to express that something is not so much effort or won't take long. The Dutch say it to lighten up the situation, make a command sound less strict or mean, ease people's minds when they are worried or show off how fast or easily they can do something. If you go to the Netherlands or Belgium, you will probably hear them say it every once in a while. Literally it means, "for a small moment" or "just for one minute."

A parent or teacher, for example, may beckon a child to come and say to a child, "Kom even hier" (Comb ay-fŭ here) instead of the harsh, commanding method of saying, "Kom hier" (Comb here).

Someone who fixes your car, can look at it and realize it will only take a minute, so you don't have to worry. He might express, "Dat doe ik even" (Dot dooh ik ay-fŭ), which means something like, "I will fix it in a few minutes, no more."

Possessive Pronouns

A possessive pronoun is a word that indicates whether something belongs to you, me, him or her, etc. Here are the possessive pronouns.

Mijn (mine) - my

Jouw/je (yow/yŭ) - your (singular)

Zijn/haar (Zine/hahr) - his/her

Ons/onze (Oans/oanzŭ) - our

Jullie (yŭ-lee) - your (plural)

Hun (hŭn) - their

However, in Dutch they don't say, "It is his" or "It is mine." Rather, they say, "It is of him" or "It is of me." Below I will show you how to say that.

Het is van mij (het is vun mye)

Het is van jou (het is vun yow)

Het is van hem/haar (het is vun hem/hahr)

Het is van ons (het is vun oans)

Het is van jullie (het is vun yŭ-lee)

Het is van hen (het is vun hen)

Chapter 4: Numbers

The Dutch numbers are pretty easy, since they are similar to the English, but once you get into the tens, like 31 or 56 or something, I have to admit the English makes a lot more sense than Dutch or German. I will explain this later. First, take a look at these.

1 (ayn) - één

2 (tway) - twee

3 (dree) - drie

4 (veer) - vier

5 (vife) - vijf

6 (zess/sess) - zes

7 (zay-fŭn) - zeven

8 (aĝt) - acht

9 (nay-ĝŭn) - negen

10 (teen) - tien

11 (elf) - elf

12 (twahlf) - twaalf

13 (der-teen) - dertien

14 (fear-teen) - veertien (whatch out, the "vier" turned into "veer")

15 (vife-teen) - vijftien

16 (zess-teen) - zestien

The others are just "zeventien" and "achttien" and "negentien." Makes sense, right?

20 (twin-tiĝ) - twintig

30 (der-tiĝ) - dertig

40 (veer-tiĝ) - veertig (here too, the "vier" became "veer")

50 (vife-tiĝ) - vijftig

60 (zess-tig) - zestig

70 (zay-fŭn-tiĝ) - zeventig

80 (taĝ-tiĝ) - tachtig (watch the extra "t" that got added in the beginning)

90 (nay-gŭn-tiĝ) - negentig

100 (hon-dŭrt) - honderd

1,000 (dow-sŭnt) - duizend

1,000,000 (mill-yoon) - miljoen

1,000,000,000 (mill-yart) - miljard [watch out, this means a billion]

Okay, so now that you know the basics, there is one more thing you need to know, and it's one of the most annoying things ever! I even think so, even though it is my proud, native language. The thing is… they don't say thirty-five, but five-and-thirty. They don't say eighty-eight, but eight-and-eighty. The Germans do it too. This only counts for tens, not for hundreds or thousands. So look at the following examples to understand it better.

75 (vife-ŭn-zay-fŭn-tiĝ) vijfenzeventig — literally: five-and-seventy

24 (fear-ŭn-twin-tiĝ) vierentwintig — literally: four-and-twenty

144 (hon-dŭrt-fear-ŭn-fear-tiĝ) honderdvierenveertig — literally: hundred-four-and-fourty

2567 (tway-dow-sŭnt-vife-hon-dŭrt-zay-fŭn-ŭn-zess-tiĝ) - tweeduizend vijfhonderd zevenenzestig — literally: two-thousand five-hundred seven-and-sixty

Pretty tricky, huh? Well, just remember to reverse the tens, and you'll be okay. After a while it becomes fairly easy. Just say three-and-twenty instead of twenty-three, etc.

Then there is the issue of "-eth." Just like in English, the first numbers are the exceptions, but after that, it's all the same add-on. At first, it's mostly "-de" and after 19, it becomes mostly "-ste." Watch below.

1st (ihr-stŭ) - eerste

2nd (tway-dŭ) - tweede

3rd (der-dŭ) - derde (so NOT "driede"; this is an exception)

4th (fear-dŭ) - vierde

5th (vife-dŭ) - vijfde

6th (zess-dŭ) - zesde

7th (zay-fŭn-dŭ) - zevende

8th (aĝ-stŭ) - achtste (exception)

9th (nay-ĝŭn-dŭ) - negende

10th (teen-dŭ) - tiende

The rest of them, like 11th, 12th, etc. have the add-on "-de." So 11, or "elf" becomes "elfde," the number 15th becomes "vijftien" + "-de" so "vijftiende," etc. When it hits 20, it becomes "-ste." So *twintigste, dertigste, veertigste,* etc. More examples:

21st (ayn-ŭn-twin-tiĝ-stŭ) - éénentwintigste

54th (fear-ŭn-five-tiĝ-stŭ) - vierenvijftigste

100th (hon-dŭrt-stŭ) - honderdste

Some other words that could be used in combination with numbers are:

keer (kear) - time — like in "the hundredth time"

procent (pro-cent) - percent

kilo (kilo) - kilo

euro (ŭro) - euro

graden Celsius (grah-dŭn) - degrees in Celsius

kilometer (keeh-loh-may-tŭr) - kilometer

de helft (dŭ helft) - half

een kwart (ŭn kwart) - a quarter of... (not the coin, but the measurement)

Time

Telling time in Dutch can be tricky. In Belgium it's more common to use the simple version Americans use, like saying that it's "twelve-thirty." A Belgian would consider it normal for you to say, "Het is twaalf uur dertig." But for people from the

Netherlands, even though they might understand it, it's not common to say it this way. Beneath are the times laid out for you, so you know what they are talking about when they say something like, "It is 10 after half three."

Hours:

12 uur (noon or midnight)

1 uur (1 o' clock)

2 uur (2 o' clock)

3 uur (etc.)

4 uur

Half hours:

12:30 - half één (literally: half one)

13:30/1:30 p.m. - half twee (literally: half two)

14:30/2:30 p.m. - half drie (etc.)

Quarterly hours:

12:15 - kwart over twaalf (quarter after twelve)

12:45 - kwart voor één (quarter to/before one)

13:15/1:15 p.m. - kwart over één (quarter after one)

Etc.

A.m. or p.m. makes no difference. If someone wants to know whether they mean a.m. or p.m., they simply add "in de ochtend" (in dŭ oĝ-tent) which means "in the morning," or "in de avond" (in dŭ ah-font) which means "in the evening." The word for "afternoon" is "middag" which literally stands for "midday."

The same principle of before and after applies to minutes, which are normally rounded up to five minutes to make it convenient. Look to the following examples:

2:40 - tien over half drie (ten after half two)

1:55 - vijf voor twee (vijf before/to two)

5:10 - tien over vijf (ten after five)

6:25 - vijf voor half zeven (five before half seven)

8:20 - tien voor half negen (ten before half nine)

10:35 - vijf over half elf (five after half eleven)

Some common expressions:

Hoe laat is het? (who laht is het?) - what time is it? — literally: How late is it?

Het is... acht uur. (het is... aĝt ure) - It is 8 o' clock.

Heb je tijd? (hep jŭ tite) - Do you have time?

horloge (whore-loh-syŭ) - watch

klok (clock) - clock

vroeg (vroog) - early

te laat (tŭ laht) - too late

op tijd (ohp tite) - on time

wanneer? (won-near?) - when?

een kwartier(tje) (ŭn kwar-teer(-tyŭ)) - a quarter of an hour/15 minutes

getal/nummer (ĝŭ-tahl/nŭm-mŭr) - number

minuut (mŭ-nute) - minute

seconde (sŭ-con-dŭ) - second

datum (dah-tŭm) - date

maand (mahnt) - month

jaar (yahr) - year

vandaag (vun-dahĝ) - today

morgen (mor-ĝŭn) - tomorrow

overmorgen (over-mor-ĝŭn) - the day after tomorrow

gisteren (ĝist-tŭ-rŭn) - yesterday

eergisteren (ere-ĝist-tŭ-rŭn) - the day before yesterday

een half uur (ŭn holf ure) - a half hour

komma (comma) - comma

punt (pŭnt) - dot/period

Side note: the Dutch, like many other European nations, reverse the commas and the periods. So the number 12,000 in Dutch would be written as 12.000; and if you talk about $5.99, a Dutch person would write is as $5,99. Try not to mess up on those.

Days of the Week

maandag (mahn-daĝ) - Monday

dinsdag (dins-daĝ) - Tuesday

woensdag (wooh-ns-daĝ) - Wednesday

donderdag (don-dŭr-daĝ) - Thursday

vrijdag (fry-daĝ) - Friday

zaterdag (sah-tŭr-daĝ) - Saturday

zondag (sohn-daĝ) - Sunday

Unlike in English, the Dutch days of the week aren't written with a capital letter, unless they are the first word of the sentence of course.

Months of the Year

The same is true for the months of the year: Unless they are the first word of the sentence, do NOT write them with a capital letter.

januari (yawn-ew-ah-ree) - January

februari (fay-brew-ah-ree) - February

maart (mahrt) - March

april (aw-pril) - April

mei (meye) - May

juni (you-nee) - June

juli (you-lee) - July (always pronounce the "l" well, since "juni" and "juli" are so close)

augustus (ouw-ĝŭs-tŭs) - August

september (september, same, just don't blow the "t") - September

oktober (october) - October

november (november, same) - November

december (day-cember) - December

The reversed principle I referred to earlier, just to make it more confusing, is also true for dates. So the date of 4/12/2015 (April 12th, 2015) would be written with dashes and with the date first, and then the month, like this: 12-4-2015. A Dutch person would say, "twaalf april tweeduizend vijftien." Other examples:

15 januari - vijftien januari (January 15th)

20 december - twintig december (December 20th)

13 juni - dertien juni (June 13th)

Chapter 5: Animals

We did a lot of grammar, some basic knowledge, and some boring stuff. I think it is interesting to study the logic of a new language and try to solve the puzzle of how their words are put together and make sense in their own way. But let's do something fun for a little while, just to give you a break. I will provide some pictures of animals and the Dutch names for them in this chapter.

Hond (hont) - dog

Kat (cot) - cat

Vogel (foh-ĝŭl) - bird

Slang (slung) - snake

Spin (spin) - spider

Vlieg (vleeĝ) - fly

Hamster (humster) - hamster

Konijn (koh-nine) - rabbit

Vis (vis) - fish

Eend (aint) - duck

Koe (khoo) - cow

Paard (pahrt) - horse

Varken (far-kŭn) - pig

Kikker (kick-kŭr) - frog

Zeehond (zay-hont) - seal (literally: Sea dog)

Vos (voas) - fox

Kip (kip) - chicken

Hert (hert) - deer

Geit (ĝite) - goat

Schaap (sĝawp) - sheep

Mier (mere) - ant

Ezel (aye-sŭl) - donkey

Hagedis (hah-ĝŭ-dis) - lizzard

Cavia (ca-vee-yah) - Guinea pig

Wolf (wohlf) - wolf

Leeuw (lay-ow) - lion

Olifant (oh-lee-funt) - elephant

Giraffe (zyee-rough) - giraffe

Zebra (zay-brah) - zebra

Nijlpaard (nile-pahrt) - hippopotamus/hippo (literally: Nile horse)

Meeuw (mee-ow) - seagull

Duif (dowf) - dove/pigeon

Tijger (tiğŭr) - tiger

Aap (ahp) - monkey

Beer (beer) - bear

Eekhoorn (akehorn) - squirrel

Dolfijn (dol-fine) - dolphin

Wasbeer (was-beer) - raccoon (literally: wash bear)

Haai (hi) - shark

Chapter 6: Body Parts

When you go to the doctor, compliment someone on his or her looks, say you get hurt, or any other situation that has to do with your body, it's handy to know what your body parts are called. So here is an overview, with an image of a happy couple.

1 haar (hahr) - hair
1 hoofd (hoaft) - head

1 brein/hersenen (brine/her-sŭ-nŭn) - brain/brains
1 schedel (sĝay-dŭl) - skull

2 wenkbrauw (wenk-brow) - eyebrow
2 voorhoofd (fore-hoaft) - forehead
2 huid (howt) - skin

3 oog (ohĝ) - eye
3 iris (ee-ris) - iris
3 pupil (pew-pil, with emphasis on "pil") - pupil
3 wimper (whim-pŭr) - eyelash

4 neus (news) - nose
4 wang (wung) - cheek

5 oor (oar) - ear
5 kaak (kawk) - jaw

6 mond (mont) - mouth
6 lippen (lip-pŭn) - lips
6 kin (kin) - chin
6 tong (tong) - tongue
6 tanden (ton-dŭn) - teeth

7 nek (neck) - neck
7 keel (cale) - throat

8 schouder (sĝow-dŭr) - shoulder

9 elleboog (el-lŭ-bowĝ) - elbow

10 buik (bowk) - belly/tummy
10 maag (mahĝ) - stomach
10 navel (nah-vŭl) - belly button/navel
10 rug (rŭĝ) - back
10 darmen (dar-mŭn) - intestines
10 blaas (blahs) - bladder

11 borsten (boar-stŭn) - breasts
11 tepel (tay-pŭl) - nipple
11 borstkas (boarst-kus) - chest

11 longen (long-ŭn) - longs
11 hart (heart) - heart
11 ribben (rib-bŭn) - ribs

12 arm (arm) - arm

13 hand (hunt) - hand
13 pols (poles) - wrist

14 vingers (fing-ŭrs) - fingers
14 nagel (nah-ĝŭl) - nail
14 knokkels (k-nock-ŭls, make sure you pronounce all "k"-s) - knuckles
14 duim (dowm) - thumb
14 wijsvinger (wise-fing-ŭr) - pointing finger
14 middelvinger (middle-fing-ŭr) - middle finger
14 ringvinger (ring-fing-ŭr) - ring finger
14 pink (pink) - pinkie

15 heup (heyp) - hip
15 billen (bill-ŭn) - butt

16 penis (pay-nŭs) - penis

17 vagina (fah-ĝee-nah) - vagina

18 knie (k-nee, pronounce the "k") - knee

19 been (bain) - leg
19 kuit (cowt) - calf

20 hiel/hak (heel/huck) - heel
20 enkel (enck-ŭl) - ankle

21 voet (foot) - foot
21 tenen (tay-nŭn) - toes

Chapter 7: Food

Just to help you order something in a restaurant or figure out what everything on the menu means, here are some key words that are connected to food and eating. You've already seen the first ten.

aardappel (awrt-opple) - potato

bloemkool (bloom-cole) - cauliflower

sinaassappel (see-nah-sup-pŭl) - orange (the fruit)

rijst (ricet) - rice

appel (up-pŭl) - apple

aardbei (ahrt-by) - strawberry

banaan (ba-nahn) - banana

water (water) - water

vis (vis) - fish

soep (soup) - soup

Now, let's teach you some new ones. Here we go.

Drinks

limonade (lee-moh-naw-dŭ) - lemonade, sugary drink or fruit drink (doesn't need to have lemon)

koffie (koh-fee) - coffee

thee (tay) - tea

wijn (wine) - wine

Meat and Fish

hamburger (hum-bŭr-ĝŭr) - hamburger

ham (hum) - ham

gehakt (ĝŭ-huckt) - minced meat

kip (kip) - chicken

vlees (flace) - meat (think of "flesh")

rundvlees (rŭnt-flace) - beef

varkensvlees (far-kŭns-flace) - pork

gehaktbal (ĝŭ-huckt-ball) - meatball

worst (wohrst) - saucage

biefstuk (beef-stŭck) - steak

garnaal (ĝar-nahl) - shrimp

zalm (zalm) - salmon

Fruit and Vegetables

broccoli (broh-coh-lee) - broccoli

bonen (bow-nŭn) - beans

fruit (frowt) - fruit

groente (ĝroon-tŭ) - vegetables

erwten (air-tŭn) - peas

maïs (mice) - corn

boerenkool (booh-rŭn-cole) - cale

wortels (wore-tŭls) - carrots

sla (slah) - lettuce

salade (sah-lah-dŭ) - salad

tomaat (toh-maht) - tomato

bosbes (boss-bess) - blueberry

braam (brahm) - blackberry

framboos (frum-bose) - raspberry

ananas (uh-nuh-nuhs) - pineapple

watermeloen (wah-tŭr-mŭ-loen) - watermelon

sperziebonen (spare-see-bow-nŭn)

abrikoos (ah-bree-cose) - apricot

nectarine (neck-tah-ree-nŭ) - nectarine

perzik (pear-sick) - peach

Spices and Seasonings

nootmuskaat (note-mŭs-kaht) - nutmeg

zout (zowt) - salt

peper (pay-pŭr) - pepper

kaneel (kuh-nail) - cinnamon

kerrie (care-ree) - curry

oregano (oar-aye-ĝah-no, with emphasis on "ĝah," contrary to the English - oregano

knoflook (knoff-loke) - garlic

tijm (time) - thyme

Other

snack (snack, same word, just don't blow the "k") - snack

ontbijt (unt-bite) - breakfast

lunch (lŭnch) - lunch

spaghetti (spah-ĝhe-tee) - spaghetti

frietjes (freet-yŭs) - (French) fries

avondeten (ah-funt-aye-tŭn) - dinner

noten (no-tŭn) - nuts

chips (ships) - chips/crisps

snoep (snoop) - candy/sweets

chocola(de) (shoh-coh-lah-dŭ) - chocolate

brood (browt) - bread

boter (bow-tŭr) - butter

jam (syem) - jam/jelly

kaas (coss) - cheese

pinda (pin-dah) - peanut

pindakaas (pin-dah-coss) - peanut butter

melk (melk) - milk

stroop (strowp) - syrup

chocopasta (sho-coh-pus-tah) - chocolate spread (for bread, like Nutella)

hagelslag (ḥah-ĝŭl-sluĝ) - chocolate sprinkles (for bread, common in the Netherlands and Belgium)

scherp (sĝearp) - sharp/spicy

heet (hate) - hot

koud (cowt) - cold

Chapter 8: Family

Family relationships matter, whether it concerns immediate family or extended family. In Dutch, they are two different words. Extended family, like aunts, uncles, nieces, nephews, cousins, etc. are called "familie" (fah-mee-lee), but if a father or mother talks about his or her family, which means partner and children, they talk about "gezin" (ĝŭ-zin). But this usually doesn't apply when a child is talking about the family he or she is in.

So, for example, you can say, "That is a happy family," referring to mother, father and children. Then you would say, "Dat is een gelukkig gezin" (Dot is ŭn ĝŭ-lŭ-ckiĝ ĝŭ-zin).

A child could say, "I come from a big family." That child would say, "Ik kom uit een groot gezin" (Ik coam out ŭn ĝrowt ĝŭ-zin), since he or she is referring to THE family he or she grew up in.

But if a child says something like, "My (immediate) family is loud," he or she would say, "Mijn familie is luidruchtig" (Mine fah-mee-lee is loud-rŭĝ-tŭĝ), since he or she is referring to the family he or she belongs to, not the one he or she presides over. I know, it's a little complicated, but just guess if you're not sure. They know what you mean. Most times, "gezin" refers to immediate family and "familie" to extended familie.

Let's go over some of the family members now, so you can get the basics.

broer (broor) - brother

zus (zŭs) - sister

vader (vah-dŭr) - father

moeder (mooh-dŭr) - mother

zoon (zone) - son

dochter (dohĝ-tŭr) - daughter

schoonbroer (sĝohn-broor) - brother in law

schoonzus (sĝohn-zŭs) - sister in law

schoonvader (sĝohn-vah-dŭr) - father in law

schoonmoeder (sĝohn-mooh-dŭr) - mother in law

schoonzoon (sĝohn-zone) - son in law

schoondochter (sĝohn-dohĝ-tŭr) - daughter in law

neef (nayf) - cousin (male)

nicht (niĝt) - cousin (female)

neefje (nayf-yŭ) - nephew

nichtje (niĝ-yŭ) - niece

vrouw (vrow) - wife/woman (don't say "wijf" since it is a degrading word for "woman")

man (mun) - husband/man

geadopteerd (ĝŭ-aw-dop-tere-t) - adopted

aangetrouwd (ahn-ĝŭ-trouwt) - married into

gescheiden (ĝŭ-sĝeye-dŭn) - divorced

ik woon samen met... (ik wohn sah-mŭn met...) - I live together with...

vriend (vreent) - boyfriend/friend (male)

vriendin (vreen-din) - girlfriend/friend (female)

verloofde (fair-low-f-dŭ) - fiancé

de oppas (dŭ ohp-poss) - the babysitter

Wil jij later veel kinderen? (Will yeye law-tŭr veil kin-dŭ-rŭn?) - Do you want a lot of kids when you grow up? (Literally: Want you later many children?)

Chapter 9: Verbs, Present Tense

Now that we've gone over some fun themes, I will show you one of the best ways to master a languages: Learning verbs. Every sentence in any language includes a verb, so memorizing the most important ones is half the work.

When it comes to verbs, there are those that follow the regular pattern. In English, those are the ones that simply add an "-s" to the he/she/it conjugation, and "-ed" to the past tense or past participle. But some don't follow that pattern, like "I fly" but in the past tense "I flew." The same is true in Dutch. Some verbs follow the common pattern and have the same letters added to them when it changes into the past tense or past participle, but others, usually the ones that get used most, are irregular. Let's take a look at a regular verb with normal and consistent conjugations that can be used as a standard for others.

For now, we are just going to focus on the present tense. The past tense will come in the other 2 books.

First, please understand what an "infinitive" is, which is the root of the verb without any conjugation. In English, this is "to..." like "to duck" or "to hit" or "to be" or "to have." In Dutch, this is always one word that ends at "-n" or, more commonly, "-en" like "bukken" or "slaan" or "zijn" or "hebben."

Another thing: When it comes to "you" (singular), there are two forms. It really doesn't matter which one you use a lot of times. There is "je" or "jij." The ONLY thing you need to remember, is that when there is a special emphasis on that word, you have to use "jij." For example, if you say, "You go away," it could be translated as "Je gaat weg" (Yŭ ĝaht weĝ) or as "Jij gaat weg" (Yi ĝaht weĝ).

But if the sentence is "Not I but you go away" the emphasis is placed on the word "you" because of the contrast. Therefore, it should be translated as "Niet ik maar jij gaat weg" (Neet ik mahr yi ĝaht weĝ).

The same counts for the word "we." You could use "we" (wŭ) or "wij" (why) in any case, except for when the emphasis is placed on that word as opposed to another; then it has to be "wij." And the same counts for "ze" and "zij," which means either "she" or "they."

Regular Verbs

In the present tense, the "you" and "he/she" person usually get a "t" at the end, and the plural forms, whether it's "we" or "you" (plural) or "they" usually gets "-en" added at the end. The double consonants are there to ensure that the sound stays short, like in the following example, where an extra "k" gets added, so the reader knows not to say a long "aaaah" and keep the "a" short.

By the way, the word "jullie" is pronounced as "yŭ-lee."

Pakken (puck-kŭn) - to get/to take

Ik pak
Jij pakt
Hij/zij pakt
Wij lopen
Jullie lopen
Zij lopen

The opposite is true too: When the vowel has to stay long, one of them gets deleted in the plural conjugations, since the Dutch consider 2 vowels unnecessary in a two-syllable word.

Lopen (low-pŭn) - to walk

Ik loop
Jij loopt
Hij/zij loopt
Wij lopen
Jullie lopen
Zij lopen

Maken (mah-kŭn) - to make

Ik maak
Jij maakt
Hij/zij maakt
Wij maken
Jullie maken
Zij maken

If there already is a "t" at the end of the verb, the Dutch consider it a little over the top to add an extra "t" so they just leave it out.

Zetten (zet-tŭn) - to put/to place

Ik zet
Jij zet
Hij/zij zet
Wij zetten
Jullie zetten
Zij zetten

When the verb ends with a "d" the Dutch DO add a "t" but they just don't say it. It would be a little weird to pronounce a word with "-d-t" as you would struggle to pronounce it and sound like a crazy person. Remember that you learned earlier that the Dutch pronounce the "d" at the end of the word like a "t" anyway. And also remember that the "b" at the end of a word is pronounced as a "p."

Worden (wore-dŭn) - to become

Ik word
Jij wordt
Hij/zij wordt
Wij worden
Jullie worden
Zij worden

If a word doesn't have an "e" before the last letter "n," the "e" doesn't get added to the plural forms either. Here are 2 common examples:

Doen (dune) - to do

Ik doe
Jij doet
Hij/zij doet
Wij doen
Jullie doen
Zij doen

Zien (zeen) - to see

Ik zie
Jij ziet
Hij/zij ziet
Wij zien

Jullie zien
Zij zien

Here are some verbs to memorize that have regular conjugations in the present tense. I will give you the first person with the unconjugated verb just to clarify how the singular forms come to existence.

Horen - ik hoor (hoar-ŭn - ik hoar) = to hear

Voelen - ik voel (fool-ŭn - ik fool) = to feel

Kijken - ik kijk (kike-ŭn - ik kike) = to look

Rennen - ik ren (ren-nŭn - ik ren) = to run

Zitten - ik zit (sit-tŭn - ik sit) = to sit

Krijgen - ik krijg (cry-ĝŭn - ik cryĝ) - to get

Kopen - ik koop (koh-pŭn - ik kohp) - to buy

Verkopen - ik verkoop (fair-koh-pŭn - ik fair-kohp) - to sell

Eten - ik eet (ay-tŭn - ik ayt) - to eat

Drinken - ik drink (drink-ŭn - ik drink) - to drink

Rijden - ik rijd (ride-ŭn - ik rite) - to ride/to drive

Fietsen - ik fiets (feets-ŭn - ik feets) - to ride a bicycle

Moeten - ik moet ["t" disappears] (moo-tŭn - ik moot) - to must/have to

Vinden - ik vind (fin-dŭn - ik fint) - to find (either by looking for it or expressing an opinion)

Irregular Verbs

Here are some irregular verbs that would come in handy if you memorized them, since they are so common in everyday language.

Komen (coh-mŭn) - to come

Ik kom
Jij komt
Hij/zij komt
Wij komen (so NOT: kommen)
jullie komen
zij komen

Gaan (ĝahn) - to go

Ik ga
Jij gaat
Hij/zij gaat
Wij gaan
Jullie gaan
Zij gaan

Hebben (heb-bŭn) - to have

Ik heb (pronounced as "ik hep")
Jij hebt (pronounced as "jij hept" etc.)
Wij hebben
Jullie hebben
Zij hebben

Zijn (zine) - to be

Ik ben
Jij bent
Hij/zij is
Wij zijn
Jullie zijn
Zij zijn

Geven (ĝay-fŭn) - to give

Ik geef
Jij geeft
Hij/zij geeft
Wij geven (notice the "f" turning into a "v")
Jullie geven
Zij geven

Mogen (moa-ĝŭn) - to may/be allowed to

Ik mag
Jij mag
Hij/zij mag
Wij mogen
Jullie mogen
Zij mogen

The Future Tense

The future tense in Dutch is really easy. The future tense is, just like in English and German, NOT a conjugation (I always get confused when they do that in Romanic languages like Spanish or French). This makes it simpler. The Dutch word for "will" or "shall" is "zullen." Here are the present tense conjugations of "zullen."

zullen (zŭl-lŭn) - will/shall

ik zal (zall) - I will

je/jij zult (zŭlt) - you will

hij/zij zal (zall) - he/she will

we/wij zullen (zŭl-lŭn) - we will

ze/zij zullen (zŭl-lŭn) - they will

we/wij zullen (zŭl-lŭn) - we will

Simply add the infinitive of the Dutch verb to that one, and you have a sentence in the future tense. For example, "Ik zal gaan" (Ik zall ĝahn) means "I will go," and "zij zullen gaan" (zye zŭl-lŭn ĝahn) means "they will go."

Chapter 10: Simple Phrases and Conjunctions

In this chapter, I will get you started with some easy phrases you can memorize, to use in everyday language and conversations.

First, let me tell you all the different ways you can ask for a confirmation after a sentence. In English, this if often done, depending on where you live, by saying "doesn't it?" or "isn't it?" or "right?" or "huh?" or (in Canada) "eh?" In Dutch, there are several ways to do this. The most common one first.

hè?
toch?
of niet/of wel?
nietwaar?
vind je niet?

Here are some more small talk sentences.

Kijk daar eens! (Kike dahr aynes!) - Hey, look over there!

Hoe oud ben je? (Who owt ben yŭ?) - How old are you?

Ik ben... jaar. (Ik ben ... yahr.) - I am... years old.

Lekker weer, hè? (Leck-ŭr weir, he?) - The weather is lovely, isn't it?

Waar ga je naartoe? (Wahr ĝah yŭ nahr-too?) - Where are you going?

Ik ga naar huis. (Ik ĝah nahr house) - I am going home.

Ik heb er genoeg van. (Ik hep air ĝŭ-nooĝ fun) - I've had enough of this.

Dankjewel. (Dunk-yŭ-well) - Thank you.

Bedankt. (Bŭ-dunkt) - Thank you.

Ik heb geld nodig. (Ik hep ĝelt noa-dŭĝ) - I need money.

Graag gedaan. (ĝrahĝ ĝŭ-dahn.) - You're welcome.

Geen dank. (ĝain dunk) - Don't mention it.

Dat staat je leuk. (Dot staht yŭ liyk.) - That looks good on you.

Wat gaaf, zeg! (Wot ĝahf, seĝ!) - That is so cool!

Ik heb geen zin meer. (Ik hep ĝain zin mere.) - I don't feel like it anymore.

Ik heb honger. (Ik hep hoanger.) - I am hungry (literally: I have hunger.)

Ik heb dorst. (Ik hep doarst.) - I am thirsty (literally: I have thirst.)

Hou op. (How owp.) - Stop it.

Wees eens stil. (Ways aynes still.) - Be quiet.

Wat zeg je? (Wot zeĝ yŭ?) - What did you say?

Ik begrijp het niet. (Ik bŭ-ĝripe het neet.) - I don't understand.

Ik weet het niet. (Ik wait het neet.) - I don't know.

Dat is gek! (Dot is ĝeck!) - That's so weird/crazy!

Mooi, toch? (Moye, towĝ?) - Beautiful, isn't it?

Zie ik je morgen? (Zee ik yŭ mor-ĝŭn?) - Will I see you tomorrow?

Tot straks. (Toat strucks) - See you later.

Ik voetbal graag. (Ik foot-ball ĝrahĝ) - I love to play soccer/football.

Ik heb een hekel aan hockey. (Ik hep ŭn hay-kŭl ahn hoackey.) - I hate hockey.

Ik blijf hier. (Ik blife hear.) - I am staying here.

Nu!/Nou! (New!/Now!) - Now!

Nog een keer! (Noaĝ ŭn kear.) - Again! (literally: Another time!)

Wat is dat? (Wot is dot?) - What is that?

Wat heb je daar? (Wot hep yŭ dahr?) - Wat have you got there?

Thanks again for buying my book. If you have a minute, please leave a positive review. You can leave your review by clicking on this link:

Leave your review here. Thank you!

I take reviews seriously and always look at them. This way, you are helping me provide you better content that you will LOVE in the future. A review doesn't have to be long, just one or two sentences and a number of stars you find appropriate (hopefully 5 of course).

Also, if I think your review is useful, I will mark it as "helpful." This will help you become more known on Amazon as a decent reviewer, and will ensure that more authors will contact you with free e-books in the future. This is how we can help each other.

DISCLAIMER: This information is provided "as is." The author, publishers and/or marketers of this information disclaim any loss or liability, either directly or indirectly as a consequence of applying the information presented herein, or in regard to the use and application of said information. No guarantee is given, either expressed or implied, in regard to the merchantability, accuracy, or acceptability of the information. The pages within this e-book have been copyrighted.

Speak Dutch

Book 2 of 3: Easy but Better

By Vincent Noot

Copyright @2015

All rights reserved. No part of this book may be reproduced in any form or by any means without permission in writing from the publisher, Vincent Noot.

If you like my book, please leave a positive review on Amazon. I would appreciate it a lot. Thanks! This is the link:

Subscribe to my blog: lifechangingebooksblog.blogspot.com

You can also visit my Facebook page.

Or you can look at my Pinterest board.

Contents:

Introduction	99
Chapter 1: Questions	101
Chapter 2: Conjunctives and Prepositions	107
Chapter 3: Verbs, Past Tense	113
Chapter 4: Past Participle	116
Chapter 5: Verbs, Exceptions	119
Chapter 6: Adjectives and Opposites	129
Chapter 7: Weather	139
Chapter 8: Travel	141
Chapter 9: Relationships and Romance	147
Chapter 10: Diminutives	150

Introduction

This book is for those who speak some Dutch, but want to learn a bit more. It goes deeper into the grammar and some more complicated phrases of the language.

For those who haven't bought the first book, let me tell you something about myself. As you might have seen from my last name (and yes, that's my actual name), I am of Dutch origin. In fact, I grew up in the Netherlands. My native language is Dutch. In the past, I have worked for a translation office (English to Dutch), and have become precise and exact at translating, correcting, reviewing, and proofing documents in both Dutch and English. Because of my experience in translation work and numerous editing jobs, and with my cultural background, I am confident to say that I will be one of the best Dutch language teachers you'll find. I will show you how to learn and master the Dutch language.

Languages don't have to be hard. It's all about understanding the structure of a language, not just memorizing thousands of words. Memorizing a dictionary will, however useful, only get you so far. Forming sentences and understanding grammar, the logic, and structure of a language is a whole study. One can only speak a language fluently by being completely imbedded in it for years. But at least with these 3 books, I can teach you the most important basics, and get you going, so that you'll be more confident in speaking up and reading or writing Dutch.

Like I mentioned in the first book, one of the best ways to learn a language is by understanding verbs. Other important words are nouns and adverbs. In this book, I will show you how the past tense of the Dutch verbs, as well as how to ask simple questions and use diminutives. You'll learn more about topics like romance, travel, and weather, common topics to talk about in everyday life. So if you are excited to learn more Dutch, "lees dan snel verder" (keep reading fast).

Chapter 1: Questions

In this chapter, you are going to learn how to form a question. It is pretty simple, but there are some rules and exceptions.

A few hundred years ago, people who spoke English, used the same or a similar system to transform a statement into a question as many other languages: They simply reversed the subject and the verb. But nowadays, English has become a little different by adding the word "do" in there, which is also true for changing a positive sentence into a negative one. See the following example:

Statement: You have cold feet

It used to be: Have you cold feet?

Now it is: Do you have cold feet?

However, Dutch, German, and many other languages have not put this odd phenomenon into their language. When they ask a question, they simply reverse the subject and the verb. So in Dutch, it would be:

Statement: Je hebt koude voeten (Yŭ hep cow-dŭ voo-tŭn)

Question: Heb je koude voeten? (Hep yŭ cow-dŭ voo-tŭn?)

If you were watching carefully, the "-t" disappeared in the question. This is because ANY time the verb appears BEFORE the word "je" (meaning: you), the "t" disappears. Another example of that is:

Je pakt het aan (Yŭ puckt het ahn)

Pak je het aan? (Puck yŭ het ahn?)

This is ONLY the case with the word "je" or the equivalent "jij."

Ik heb besloten mijn haar kort te laten knippen. (Ik hep bŭ-sloa-tŭn mine hahr court tŭ knip-pŭn.) - I have decided to cut my hair short.

Waarom? Lang haar is toch mooier? (Wah-rom? Lung hahr is toĝ moy-ŭr?) - Why? Isn't long hair more beautiful?

Nee. Het schijnt dat bij sommige meisjes kort haar juist beter staat. (Nay. Het sĝinet dot by som-miĝ-ŭ mye-syŭs court hahr yiyest bay-tŭr staht.) - No. It appears with some girls, short hair looks better.

Oh. Dat wist ik niet. (Oh. Dot wist ik neet.) - Oh. I didn't know that. (Literally: That knew I not.)

Hee! Ben jij een jongen of een meisje? (Hey! Ben yiye ŭn young-ŭn of ŭn mye-syŭ?) - Hey! Are you a boy or a girl?

Here are other words you should study for a little while in order to ask questions in Dutch.

Wanneer? (whun-near?) - when?

Waar? (wahr?) - where?

Wie? (wee?) - who?

Wat? (wot?) - what? (remember: Don't blow the "t")

Welke? (well-kŭ?) - which?

Waarom? (wah-rom?) - Why?

Hoe? (who?) - How? (remember to pronounce the vowel shortly)

With these words memorized, you are armed with a firm basis of asking Dutch questions. Simply combine them with the words you already know, reverse the verb and the subject, and tadaah! You have a Dutch question. Here are some common ones, just to clear it up and give you some examples.

Waar is de w.c.? (Wahr is dŭ way say?) - Where are the restrooms? ("W.c." stands for "water closed," but the word "toilet" pronounced as "twah-let" is also correct.)

Hoe gaat het? (Who gaht het?) - How are you? (Literally: How goes it?)

Waarom doe je dat? (Wah-rom do yŭ dot?) - Why are you doing that?

Welke wil je? (Well-kŭ will yŭ?) - Which one do you want?

Wie gaat er mee? (Wee gaht air may?) - Who is coming?

Waar ga je naartoe? (Wahr ĝa yŭ nahr-too) - Where are you going?

Wat is dit? (Wot is dit?) - What is this?

Hoe doe je dat? (Who do yŭ dot?) - How do you do that?

Wie ben je? (Wee ben yŭ?) - Who are you?

Waar doet het pijn? (Wahr doot het pine?) - Where does it hurt? (Literally: Where does it pijn?)

Hoe laat vertrekt de trein? (Who laht fair-trekt dŭ trine?) - What time does the train leave? (Literally: How late leaves the train?)

Waarom zeg je niks? (Wah-rom zeĝ yŭ niks?) - Why aren't you saying anything?

Wat zal ik doen? (Wot zoll ik doon?) - What shall I do?

Wanneer verhuis je? (Won-near fair-house yŭ?) - When are you moving?

Wanneer is het voorbij? (Won-near is het four-bye?) - When is it over?

Hoe laat kom je terug? (Who laht comb yŭ trŭĝ?) - What time are you coming back?

Of course that's not all there is, so let me give you a few common combinations, so you can ask more advanced questions when you really need to know something?

Wat voor...? (wot for?) - what kind of...?

Hoe vaak? (who vahk?) - how often?/how many times? (Sometimes the Dutch say, "Hoeveel keer..." in which "keer" means "times".)

Hoeveel? (who-vale?) - how much?/how many? [yes, you saw that right... it's ONE word]

Waar... vandaan? (wahr... von-dahn?) - from where?

Waar... heen? (wahr... hane?) - Whereto?

The words "waarvandaan" and "waarheen" get split up, so that the last part ("-vandaan" or "-heen") gets pushed all the way to the back of the sentence. Usually the words waar vandaan" and "waar heen" are consecutively followed by a conjugation of "komen" (to come) or "gaan" (to go). Makes sense, right?

Check out the following examples:

Hoeveel kost het? (Who-vale coast het?) - How much does it cost?

Hoeveel wil je er? (Who-vale will yŭ air?) - How many do you want?

Hoeveel maanden blijf je? (Who-vale mahn-dŭn blife yŭ?) - How many months are you staying?

Hoe vaak ga je winkelen? (Who vahk gah yŭ wink-ŭ-lŭn?) - Hoe often do you go shopping?

Hoeveel keer kun je opdrukken? (Who vale kear kŭn yŭ oap-drŭck-kŭn?) - How many push ups can you do?

Waar kom je vandaan? (Wahr comb yŭ von-dahn?) - Where are you from?

Waar gaat hij heen? (Wahr ĝaht high hane?) - Where is he going? (Side note: another way to say "waar... heen" is "waar... naartoe")

Chapter 2: Conjunctives and Prepositions

A conjunctive puts two sentences together, and a preposition puts two words or parts of a sentence together. Here are some of the most important words to remember to form more complicated sentences:

Conjunctives

En ("end" without the "d") - and

Of (of) - or

Maar (mahr) - but

Dus (dŭs) - so

Als (oals) - if/when

Omdat (oam-dot) - because

Want (wunt) - because

Zodat (sow-dot) - so that

Nadat (nah-dot) - after

Voordat (fore-dot) - before

Sinds (sints) - since

Toen (tune) - then/when (as in, "When I did that, I started to...")

Tot(dat) (toat-[dot]) - until

Behalve (bŭ-hall-vŭ) - except for

Tenzij (ten-sigh) - unless

Alsof (oals-of) - as if

Hoewel (who-well) - although

Examples:

Hij zei iets voordat hij aankwam. (High zigh eets fore-dot high ahn-kwom) - He said something before he arrived

Ik ben blij, want ik heb veel geld. (Ik ben bleye, wunt ik hep veil ĝelt) - I am happy, because I have lots of money.

Als het goed is, ga ik ermee akkoord. (Oals het ĝoot is, ĝah ik air-may ak-koart) - If it is good, I will agree.

Hij is thuis en hij is boos. (High is thouse en high is bose) - He is home and he is angry.

Het klinkt leuk, maar ik weet het niet. (Het klinkt leyk, mahr ik wait het neet) - It sounds like fun, but I don't know.

Wil je deze of die hebben? (Will yŭ day-sŭ of dee heb-bŭn?) - Do you want to have this one or that one?

Ik werk hard, zodat ik genoeg heb. (Ik werk hart, so-dot ik ĝŭ-nooĝ hep) - I work hard, so that I will have enough.

Ik wacht totdat je er bent (Ik wuĝt toat-dot yŭ air bent) - I will wait until you are there.

As you may have noticed, in some of these sentences, the verb gets switched around or pushed towards the back of the sentence. This is called "inversion" which I will discuss in the 3rd book:

Speak Dutch: Book 3 of 3: Advanced

Prepositions

Aan (ahn) - on

Op (oap) - on/at

Uit (out) - out/off

Met (met) - with

In (in) - in

Van (vun) - of/from

Volgens (voal-ĝŭns) - according to

Voor (for) - for/in front of

Via (vee-ah) - via

Zonder (soan-dŭr) - without

Bij (by) - by/at

Binnen (bin-nŭn) - inside

Buiten (bow-tŭn) - outside

Door (door) - through/by

Over (over) - over

Tegenover (tay-ĝŭn-over) - across from

Tussen (tŭs-sŭn) - in between

Onder (oan-dŭr) - under

Achter (uĝ-tŭr) - behind

Boven (bow-fŭn) - above

Naast (nahst) - next to

Naar (nahr) - to (as in: in the direction of...)

Not prepositions but good to know

Links (Lings) - left [don't pronounce the "k"]

Rechts (reĝts [in some dialects without the "t"]) - right

Kant (kunt [yep, that's how you say it... sorry. Just don't blow the "k" or the "t" and you're good]) - side

Linkerkant (lin-kŭr-kunt) - left side

Rechterkant (reĝ-tŭr-kunt) - right side

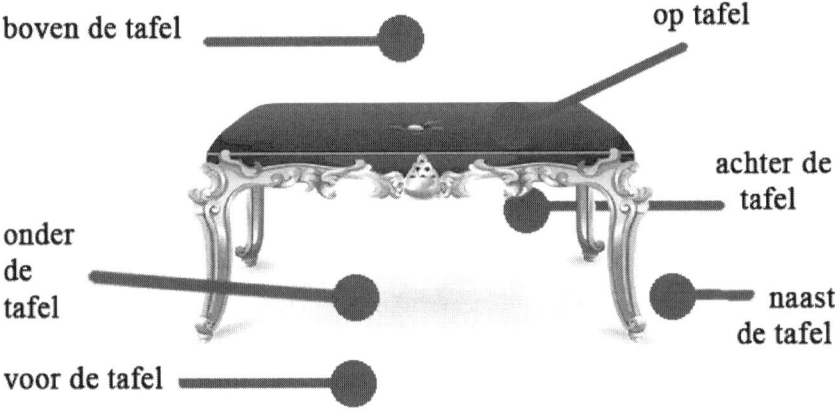

When it comes to the table in particular, there is a standard expression that says, "op tafel." In that exceptions, de word "de" is often left out.

You might have seen the name "van..." before or you may know someone who has that word in his last name. It comes from the time that people often made up last names referring to the city they were born in. A last name like "van Bergen" simply means that their ancestors came from the Dutch town Bergen. Of course not every Dutch last name has that word, but if you open up the phone book in any town in the Netherlands or Belgium, you would see a lot of last names that start with "van...."

Here are some examples of sentences in which the above-mentioned prepositions exist:

Trek je kleren aan. (Treck yŭ clear-ŭn ahn) - Put your clothes on. ["trekken" means "to pull" so literally: "Pull your clothes on.")

Doe het licht uit. (Doo het liĝt out) - Turn the light off.

Friet met mayonnaise. (Freet met mah-yo-naih-sŭ) - fries with mayonnaise (more common than with ketchup in the Netherlands and Belgium; I encourage you to try it.)

Ik ga zonder hem weg. (Ik ĝah soan-dŭr hem weĝ) - I am going away/leaving without him.

Ik heb een pet op mijn hoofd. (Ik hep ŭn pet op mine hoaft) - I have a hat on my head.

Ligt je broek op de bank? (Liĝt yŭ brook op dŭ bunk?) - Are your pants on the couch/sofa?

Ik ga morgen naar buiten. (Ik ĝah mor-ĝŭn noar bow-tŭn) - Tomorrow I will go outside.

Volgens mij is dat verkeerd. (Foal-ĝŭns mye is dot fair-keart) - I think that is wrong. (Literally: "According to me is that wrong." The Dutch use "volgens mij" a lot when they are saying "I think that...."

Ze gaat naar de dokter. (Zŭ ĝaht nahr dŭ dock-tŭr) - She is going to the doctor.

Ik sta voor de deur. (Ik stah four dŭ dŭr) - I am standing at the door/in front of the door.

Ik loop door de deur. (Ik lohp door dŭ dŭr) - I am walking through the door.

Dat ding is van mij! (Dot ding is vun mye!) - That thing is mine!

Ik heb een cadeau voor je. (Ik hep ŭn kah-dow four yŭ) - I have a gift/present for you.

Dat is aardig van je. (Dot is ahr-dŭĝ vun yŭ) - That is nice of you.

Ik rijd via Amsterdam. (Ik rite vee-ah Um-stŭr-dum) - I am driving via Amsterdam.

Hij staat achter me, of niet? (High staht uĝ-tŭr mŭ, of neet?) - He is standing right behind me, isn't he?

We rijden nu door de tunnel. (Wŭ ridŭn new door dŭ tŭn-nŭl) - We are now driving through the tunnel.

Chapter 3: Verbs, Paste Tense

In English, most verbs in the past tense end with "-d" or with "-ed" but in Dutch it's a bit more complicated, unfortunately. Not by much, but still...

In this chapter, I will show you how to conjugate regular verbs.

Verbs with "-t" in the Past Tense

There are two kinds of regular verbs in the past tense. There are lots of exceptions, but those are irregular and we'll go into those later. I will give you an example, so you can understand the model which a decent percentage of the Dutch verbs in the past tense follow. First, let's do one with the short vowel sound in the first syllable.

Pakken (puck-kŭn) - to take

ik pakte (ik puck-tŭ) - I took
jij pakte (yeye puck-tŭ) - you took (singular)
hij/zij pakte (hye/zye puck-tŭ) - he/she took
wij pakten (wye puck-tŭn) - we took
jullie pakten (yŭ-lee puck-tŭn) - you took (plural)
zij pakten (zye puck-tŭn) - they took

Simple, right? Just add "-te" in the singular form or "-ten" in the plural form and you're done. Actually, since the Dutch often slack off the "-n" at the end, the plural form often sounds like the singular form anyway, so if you're not sure, just don't pronounce the "-n" at the end and you're good.

Here is an example of the verbs with long vowels in the first syllable. It's really easy if you think about the logic behind the short and long sounds and the way they are spelled.

Note that the letter "v" often turns into an "f" and the letter "z" often turns into an "s."

Raken (rah-kŭn) - to touch

ik raakte (ik rahk-tŭ) - I touched
jij raakte (yeye rahk-tŭ) - you touched (singular)
hij/zij raakte (hye/zye rahk-tŭ) - he/she touched
wij raakten (wye rahk-tŭn) - we touched
jullie raakten (yŭ-lee rahk-tŭn) - you touched (plural)
zij raakten (zye rahk-tŭn) - they touched

Verbs that follow this pattern are, for instance:

Schoppen (schopte) - to kick

Fietsen (fietste) - to ride a bike

Zetten (zette) - to put/place

Plaatsen (plaatste) - to place

Werken (werkte) - to work

Maken (maakte) - to make

Beven (beefte) - to shake/shiver

Kleven (kleefte) - to cleave/stick

Plakken (plakte) - to paste/glue

Verbs with a "-d" in the PastTense

The verbs with "-d" in the past tense follow the same logic. It's not that hard to figure them out. The only flaw is that, unfortunately, it's not always simple to find out whether a verbs follows the "-t" or the "-d" pattern. There are certain consonants that are often followed by a "-d" in the past tense and certain ones that are often followed by a "-t" in the past tense, but going over all the consonants in every case may even confuse your brain more than just trying to remember which one belongs to which verb and developing a feeling for the language that way, so I won't bother you with that information too much. It basically comes down to the fact that the letters T, K, F, S, CH, P are usually followed by a "-t" and the rest by a "-d."

Vullen (vŭl-lŭn) - to fill

ik vulde (ik vŭl-dŭ) - I filled
jij vulde (yeye vŭl-dŭ) - you filled (singular)
hij/zij vulde (hye/zye vŭl-dŭ) - he/she filled
wij vulden (wye vŭl-dŭn) - we filled
jullie vulden (yŭ-lee vŭl-dŭn) - you filled (plural)
zij vulden (zye vŭl-dŭn) - they filled

Verbs that more or less follow this pattern are, for instance:

Antwoorden (antwoordde) - to answer

Horen (hoorde) - to hear

Rennen (rende) - to run

Verven (verfde) - to paint

Willen (wilde) - to want

Leggen (legde) - to lay/put

Chapter 4: Past Participle

Verbs with "-t" in the Past Tense

Again, there are two kinds of regular verbs in the past tense, one with the "-t" and another with the "-d" ending. The same counts for the past participle. First, let's do one with the short vowel sound in the first syllable.

Pakken (puck-kŭn) - to take

ik heb gepakt (ik hep (ĝŭ-puckt)

See? It's easy. You just take the root or stem from the word, add a "-t" or "-d" at the end, and you add "ge-" in front of it. I will show you through the examples from the previous chapter how simple it is when it comes to the regular verbs.

With a "-t"

Schoppen - geschopt

Fietsen - gefietst

Zetten - gezet (NEVER dubbel "t" at the end)

Plaatsen - geplaatst

Werken - gewerkt

Maken - gemaakt

Beven - gebeeft

Kleven - gekleeft

Plakken - geplakt

With a "-d" (still pronounced as a "-t")

Antwoorden - geantwoord

Horen - gehoord

Rennen - gerend

Verven - geverfd

Willen - gewild

So here is the thing: The Dutch never pronounce a "d" at the end as a "d," but always as a "t." So "ik heb gerend" is pronounced as "ik hep ĝŭ-rent" etcetera.

"Ver-" and "her-" and stuff

Some of the prepositions that we add to words, just like in English, come from Latin. The Dutch think it's silly to add "ge-" at the beginning, since the 2 or 3 letters in the word are already something that's added on. So look at the following patterns when it comes to these words. If you see anything similar with the same first few letters in the verb, it usually means you don't add "ge-" to the past participle.

First, the verb, then the past participle (in brackets) and then the translation:

Verwennen (ik heb verwend) - I have spoiled (of course "I am spoiled" is "Ik ben verwend" in Dutch)

Beroven (ik heb beroofd) - I have robbed

Beloven (ik heb beloofd) - I have promised

Herkennen (ik heb herkend) - I have recognized

Verpakken (ik heb verpakt) - I have wrapped (a gift)

Chapter 5: Verbs, Exceptions

In this chapter, I will show you how to conjugate irregular verbs, the exceptions. Some people have said that German is all about rules and Dutch is all about exceptions, which doesn't make it easy for foreigners to learn and to memorize each single one.

The funny thing is that it might be related to the culture. Whenever I am in Germany, I feel like many people follow the rules, come on time, and have forms and procedures for everything. When I lived in Belgium, I felt like more people avoided conflict, cared about politeness and hierarchy, and had a certain way of esteeming others as having a higher status or position. When I lived in the Netherlands, I got the feeling people were very forward, cared more about the underlying reasons of rules, and were willing to bend them at times or consider others as equals, often speaking their minds and saying what everyone else was thinking. And I guess the language, with all its exceptions, followed the culture.

Here I will show some of the main ones, so you can have a basic understanding of what to say when speaking Dutch and wanting to talk in the past tense. So good luck memorizing all these! I wish I could show you a trick, but that's just the trouble with Dutch. As you discover patterns and speak the language more often, you'll get more of a feel for it, so then, the exceptions will be easier, but I have to say that it is probably still challenging for a foreigner.

Jee! Werkwoorden uit het hoofd leren...

Yay! Memorizing verbs... (Literally: "Work-words out the head learn....")

Ja, vervelend, man!

Yes, annoying, man!

Remember: The conjugations below are ALL in the past tense. The last one is the past participle!

Zijn - to be

ik was (ik was)
jij was (yeye was)
hij/zij was (hye/zye was)
wij waren (wye wah-rŭn)

jullie waren (yŭ-lee wah-rŭn)
zij waren (zye wah-rŭn)
Ik ben geweest (ik ben ĝŭ-waist)

Hebben - to have

ik had (ik hut)
jij had (yeye hut)
hij/zij had (hye/zye hut)
wij hadden (wye hu-dŭn)
jullie hadden (yŭ-lee hu-dŭn)
zij hadden (zye hu-dŭn)
Ik heb gehad (ik hep ĝŭ-hut)

Vragen - to ask

ik vroeg (ik frooĝ)
jij vroeg (yeye frooĝ)
hij/zij vroeg (hye/zye frooĝ)
wij vroegen (wye frooĝ-ŭn)
jullie vroegen (yŭ-lee frooĝ-ŭn)
zij vroegen (zye frooĝ-ŭn)
Ik heb gevraagd (ik hep ĝŭ-frahĝt)

Lopen - to walk

Ik liep (ik leap)
jij liep (yeye leap)
hij/zij liep (hye/zye leap)
wij liepen (wye lea-pŭn)
jullie liepen (yŭ-lee lea-pŭn)
zij liepen (zye lea-pŭn)
Ik heb gelopen (ik hep ĝŭ-loa-pŭn)

Slaan - to hit/punch

ik stond (ik stoant)
jij stond (yeye stoant)
hij/zij stond (hye/zye stoant)
wij stonden (wye stoan-dŭn)
jullie stonden (yŭ-lee stoan-dŭn)
zij stonden (zye stoan-dŭn)
Ik heb gestaan (ik hep ĝŭ-stahn)

Kijken - to look

ik keek (ik cake)
jij keek (yeye cake)
hij/zij keek (hye/zye cake)
wij keken (wye cay-kŭn)
jullie keken (yŭ-lee cay-kŭn)
zij keken (zye cay-kŭn)
Ik heb gekeken (ik hep ĝŭ-cay-kŭn)

Zien - to see

ik zag (ik suĝ)
jij zag (yeye suĝ)
hij/zij zag (hye/zye suĝ)
wij zagen (wye sah-ĝŭn)
jullie zagen (yŭ-lee sah-ĝŭn)
zij zagen (zye sah-ĝŭn)
Ik heb gezien (ik hep ĝŭ-seen)

Weten - to know

ik wist (ik wist)
jij wist (yeye wist)
hij/zij wist (hye/zye wist)
wij wisten (wye wist-ŭn)
jullie wisten (yŭ-lee wist-ŭn)
zij wisten (zye wist-ŭn)
Ik heb geweten (ik hep ĝŭ-way-tŭn)

Kunnen - to can/be able to

ik kon (ik cone [but short vowel])
jij kon (yeye cone [but short vowel])
hij/zij kon (hye/zye cone [but short vowel])
wij konden (wye cone-dŭn [but short vowel])
jullie konden (yŭ-lee cone-dŭn [but short vowel])
zij konden (zye cone-dŭn [but short vowel])
Ik heb gekund (ik hep ĝŭ-kŭnt)

Zoeken - to search/seek/look for

Ik zocht (ik soĝt)
jij zocht (yeye soĝt)
hij/zij zocht (hye/zye soĝt)
wij zochten (wye soĝt-ŭn)
jullie zochten (yŭ-lee soĝt-ŭn)
zij zochten (zye soĝt-ŭn)
Ik heb gezocht (ik hep ĝŭ-soĝt)

Notice how "kopen" follows the same pattern as "zoeken" even though the vowels are different in the present tense:

Kopen - to buy/purchase

Ik kocht (ik koĝt)
jij kocht (yeye koĝt)
hij/zij kocht (hye/zye koĝt)
wij kochten (wye koĝt-ŭn)
jullie kochten (yŭ-lee koĝt-ŭn)
zij kochten (zye koĝt-ŭn)
Ik heb gekocht (ik hep ĝŭ-koĝt)

Krijgen - to get/receive

ik kreeg (ik crayĝ)
jij kreeg (yeye crayĝ)

hij/zij kreeg (hye/zye crayĝ)
wij kregen (wye crayĝ-ŭn)
jullie kregen (yŭ-lee crayĝ-ŭn)
zij kregen (zye crayĝ-ŭn)
Ik heb gekregen (ik hep ĝŭ-crayĝ-ŭn)

Spreken - to speak

ik sprak (ik spruck)
jij sprak (yeye spruck)
hij/zij sprak (hye/zye spruck)
wij spraken (wye sprah-ckŭn)
jullie spraken (yŭ-lee sprah-ckŭn)
zij spraken (zye sprah-ckŭn)
Ik heb gesproken (ik hep ĝŭ-sproa-ckŭn)

Zitten - to sit

ik zat (ik sut)
jij zat (yeye sut)
hij/zij zat (hye/zye sut)
wij zaten (wye sah-tŭn)
jullie zaten (yŭ-lee sah-tŭn)
zij zaten (zye sah-tŭn)
Ik heb gezeten (ik hep ĝŭ-say-tŭn)

Zeggen - to say

Ik zei (ik zye)
jij zei (yeye zye)
hij/zij zei (hye/zye zye)
wij zeiden (wye zye-dŭn)
jullie zeiden (yŭ-lee zye-dŭn)
zij zeiden (zye zye-dŭn)
Ik heb gezegd (ik hep ĝŭ-seĝt)

Gaan - to go

ik ging (ik ĝing)
jij ging (yeye ĝing)
hij/zij ging (hye/zye ĝing)
wij gingen (wye ĝing-ŭn)
jullie gingen (yŭ-lee ĝing-ŭn)
zij gingen (zye ĝing-ŭn)
Ik ben gegaan (ik ben ĝŭ-ĝahn)

Komen - to come

Ik kwam (ik kwum)
jij kwam (yeye kwum)
hij/zij kwam (hye/zye kwum)
wij kwamen (wye kwah-mŭn)
jullie kwamen (yŭ-lee kwah-mŭn)
zij kwamen (zye kwah-mŭn)
Ik ben gekomen (ik ben ĝŭ-koa-mŭn)

Trekken - to pull

ik trok (ik trock)
jij trok (yeye trock)
hij/zij trok (hye/zye trock)
wij trokken (wye troa-ckŭn [short vowel])
jullie trokken (yŭ-lee troa-ckŭn [short vowel])
zij trokken (zye troa-ckŭn [short vowel])
Ik heb getrokken (ik hep ĝŭ-troa-ckŭn [short vowel])

Brengen - to bring

ik bracht (ik bruĝt)
jij bracht (yeye bruĝt)
hij/zij bracht (hye/zye bruĝt)
wij brachten (wye bruĝt-ŭn)
jullie brachten (yŭ-lee bruĝt-ŭn)

zij brachten (zye bruĝt-ŭn)
Ik heb gebracht (ik hep ĝŭ- bruĝt)

Doen - to do

ik deed (ikd date)
jij deed (yeye date)
hij/zij deed (hye/zye date)
wij deden (wye day-dŭn)
jullie deden (yŭ-lee day-dŭn)
zij deden (zye day-dŭn)
Ik heb gedaan (ik hep ĝŭ-dahn)

Drinken - to drink

ik dronk (ik droank [pronounced shortly])
jij dronk (yeye droank [pronounced shortly])
hij/zij dronk (hye/zye droank [pronounced shortly])
wij dronken (wye droank-ŭn [pronounced shortly])
jullie dronken (yŭ-lee droank-ŭn [pronounced shortly])
zij dronken (zye droank-ŭn [pronounced shortly])
Ik heb gedronken (ik hep ĝŭ-droank-ŭn [pronounced shortly])

Eten - to eat

ik at (ik ot [like in "hot"])
jij at (yeye ot)
hij/zij at (hye/zye ot)
wij aten (wye ah-tŭn)
jullie aten (yŭ-lee ah-tŭn)
zij aten (zye ah-tŭn)
Ik heb gegeten (ik hep ĝŭ-ĝay-tŭn)

Geven - to give

ik gaf (ik ĝof)
jij gaf (yeye ĝof)

hij/zij gaf (hye/zye ĝof)
wij gaven (wye ĝah-fŭn)
jullie gaven (yŭ-lee ĝah-fŭn)
zij gaven (zye ĝah-fŭn)
Ik heb gegeven (ik hep ĝŭ-ĝay-fŭn)

Helpen - to help

ik hielp (ik heelp)
jij hielp (yeye heelp)
hij/zij hielp (hye/zye heelp)
wij hielpen (wye heel-pŭn)
jullie hielpen (yŭ-lee heel-pŭn)
zij hielpen (zye heel-pŭn)
Ik heb geholpen (ik hep ĝŭ-hoal-pŭn)

Mogen - to may/be allowed to

ik mocht (ik moaĝt [short vowel])
jij mocht (yeye moaĝt [short vowel])
hij/zij mocht (hye/zye moaĝt [short vowel])
wij mochten (wye moaĝt-ŭn [short vowel])
jullie mochten (yŭ-lee moaĝt-ŭn [short vowel])
zij mochten (zye moaĝt-ŭn [short vowel])
Ik heb gemogen (ik hep ĝŭ-mow-ĝŭn [long vowel])

Slapen - to sleep

ik sliep (ik sleep)
jij sliep (yeye sleep)
hij/zij sliep (hye/zye sleep)
wij sliepen (wye sleepŭn)
jullie sliepen (yŭ-lee sleepŭn)
zij sliepen (zye sleepŭn)
Ik heb geslapen (ik hep ĝŭ-slah-pŭn)

Springen - to jump

ik sprong (ik sprong)
jij sprong (yeye sprong)
hij/zij sprong (hye/zye sprong)
wij sprongen (wye sprong-ŭn)
jullie sprongen (yŭ-lee sprong-ŭn)
zij sprongen (zye sprong-ŭn)
Ik heb gesprongen (ik hep ĝŭ-sprong-ŭn)

Vallen - to fall

Ik viel (ik feel)
jij viel (yeye feel)
hij/zij viel (hye/zye feel
wij vielen (wye feel-ŭn)
jullie vielen (yŭ-lee feel-ŭn)
zij vielen (zye feel-ŭn)
Ik ben gevallen (ik ben ĝŭ-fall-ŭn)

Worden - to become

ik werd (ik wert)
jij werd (yeye wert)
hij/zij werd (hye/zye wert)
wij werden (wye wer-dŭn)
jullie werden (yŭ-lee wer-dŭn)
zij werden (zye wer-dŭn)
Ik heb geworden (ik hep ĝŭ-woar-dŭn)

Chapter 6: Adjectives

Adjectives are words that describe something, like beautiful, high, ugly, stupid, smart, interesting, boring, etc.

After learning 6 languages and speaking some of them pretty fluently, I have concluded that the best way to learn adjectives, is to always learn opposites. If you learn the word "big," it's better to immediately learn what "small" is in that same language. If you learn the word "far," it would be best to know how to say "close" at the same time.

On the other hand, if you really don't know the opposite word, just say what it is not. For example, if you memorized the word "lang" (meaning: long) but you forgot the word "kort" (meaning: short), you can use that. Just say, "niet lang" (not long), or in other words: Short.

Okay, enough chit-chat. Ready? Here we go.

kort (court) - short
lang (long) - long

gek (ĝeck) - crazy
raar (rahr) - weird
normaal (nor-mahl [emphasis on "maal") - normal
gewoon (ĝŭ-wone) - sane/normal/regular

dom (domb) - stupid/dumb
slim (slim) - smart

knap (knupp) - handsome/pretty
mooi (moye) - beautiful/pretty
lelijk (lay-lŭck) - ugly
sexy (sexy) - sexy
schattig (sĝu-tiĝ) - cute

groot (ĝroht) - big/large
klein (kline) - small/little

ver (fair) - far
dichtbij (diĝt-by) - close

dun (dŭn) - thin
dik (dick [don't blow the "k"]) - fat/thick

gespierd (ĝŭ-speert) - muscled/buff
sterk (stairck) - strong
zwak (zwuck) - weak

blij (blye) - happy
boos (bose) - angry
verdrieting (fair-dree-tiĝ) - sad

rijk (ricke) - rich
arm (arm) - poor

leuk (leyk) - fun
grappig (ĝrap-piĝ) - funny
stom (stoam) - stupid
saai (sye) - boring

goed (goot) - good
slecht (sleĝt) - bad

wijd (wite) - wide
smal (small) - narrow
breed (brait) - wide

ingewikkeld (in ĝŭ-wick-ŭlt) - complicated
simpel (simple) - simple
eenvoudig (ayn-fow-dŭg) - simple

makkelijk (muck-kŭ-lŭck) - easy
moeilijk (mooy-lŭck) - hard/difficult

moe (mooh) - tired
opgewonden (op-ĝŭ-woan-dŭn) - excited
enthousiast (ent-how-see-ust) - enthusiastic
energiek (ay-nŭr-zyeeck) - energetic

gefrustreerd (ĝŭ-frŭs-treert) - frustrated
kalm (calm) - calm

lui (louw) - lazy
ijverig (ive-ŭ-riĝ) - diligent (often they say, "werkt hard" [works hard])

gemeen (ĝŭ-main) - mean
aardig (ahr-diĝ) - nice
vriendelijk (freen-dŭ-lŭck) - friendly

lief (leef) - sweet
stout (stout) - naughty

handig (hun-diĝ) - handy
onhandig (oan-hun-diĝ) - unhandy/clumsy

nat (nut) - wet
vochtig (foaĝ-tiĝ)
droog (droĝue) - dry

koud (cowt) - cold
warm (wurm) - warm
heet (hate) - hot

vaag (fahĝ) - vague
duidelijk (dow-dŭ-lŭck) - clear

lekker (leck-ŭr) - tasty/delicious
vies (fees) - dirty/disgusting
schoon (sĝone) - clean (in the Flemish dialect in Belgium, it often means "beautiful." The word "proper" is often used for "clean" there.)

eerlijk (eer-lŭck) - honest
oneerlijk (oan-eer-lŭck) - dishonest

hard (heart) - hard
zacht (soĝt) - soft

kapot (kah-pot) - broken
stuk (stŭck) - broken

heel (hail) - whole
intact (in-tuckt) - intact

hoog (hoĝue) - high
laag (laĝue) - low

duur (dure) - expensive
goedkoop (ĝoot-cope) - cheap (literally: good buy)

Other helpful stuff:

Niet... genoeg (Neet... ĝŭ-nooĝ) - Not... enough

Te... (Tŭ) - Too...

3 words for "very":

Heel (hail) - very

Erg (airĝ) - very

Zeer (zear) - very

Some examples of sentences with adjectives:

Nee, je rijdt te snel! (Nay, yŭ ĝaht tŭ snell) - No, you are driving too fast!

Die hamer is handig. (Dee hah-mŭr is hun-dŭĝ.) - That hamer is handy.

Blijf kalm. Het komt wel goed. (Blife calm. Het combt well ĝoot.) - Stay calm. It's going to be okay.

Wat een mooi meisje! (Wot ŭn moy mye-syŭ!) - What a beautiful girl!

Harder werken! Niet lui zijn! (Harder where-kŭn! Neet louw sine!) - Work harder! Don't be lazy!

Ik ben lief. Jij bent stout. (Ik ben leef. Yiye bent stout.) - I am sweet/nice. You are naughty/bad.

Conjugating Adjectives

The hardest thing about adjectives in Dutch is that they go along with the article and noun they belong to. If you don't know and you have to guess, just add an "e" to it and you are more likely to pronounce it correctly. But for those who want to learn it more precisely, here are some general guidelines.

By itself it does NOT have an "e"

If the adjective isn't attached to a noun, it NEVER has an "e" at the end. For example: "Ik ben groot." (I am big). In this case, there is no noun. Another example is: "Ze is heel klein." (She is very small).

Het and De and Een

When the article of the noun is "het," the adjective OFTEN has an "e" at the end. For example: "Het grote boek." (The big book.) The letter "o" disappears, since the pronunciation of the long sound stays the same. Therefore it is pronounced as "Het ĝroa-tŭ book."

When the article of the noun is "de," the adjective ALWAYS has an "e" at the end. For example: "De grote pan." (The big pan.)

When the article of the noun is "een" but the original article belonging to that noun is "de," the adjective ALWAYS has an "e" too. For example "Een grote pan" (since it is "de pan".)

When the article of the noun is "een" but the original article belonging to that noun is "het" it CAN have an "e." This is true in most cases. For example: "Een groot boek" (since it is "het boek").

More examples:

Een groot huis (a big house)

Een mooie tuin (a beautiful yard/garden)

De aardige jongen (a nice boy)

Het grappige kind (the funny child)

Een leuke buurman (a fun neighbor)

Een knappe man (a handsome man)

De harde tafel (the hard table)

Een mooi meisje (a pretty girl)

Het kapotte ding (the broken thing)

Een grote doos (a big box)

De dikke dokter (the fat doctor)

Een kleine kist (a small chest)

Een hoge boom (a high tree)

Superlative Stuff

The similarity in Dutch and English lies in the fact that if something is bigger, better, or more powerful, even if something is the highest, tallest, greatest... the Dutch has the same endings. See for example:

Groot - groter - grootst

Klein - kleiner - kleinste

Grappig - grappiger - grappigst

Mooi - mooier - mooiste

Lelijk - lelijker - lelijkst

Laag - lager - laagst

Of course, the annoying thing is they need an "e" at the end sometimes, just like with all adjectives, if it applies to the noun and the article belonging to it. For instance:

Het grootste boek (the biggest book)

Het mooiste huis (the most beautiful house/home)

Een lagere boom (a lower tree)

De knapste dochter (the prettiest daughter)

A Couple Exceptions

Goed - beter - best (good - better - best)

Veel - meer - meest (veel - meer - meest)

Examples:

Ik heb meer dan jij. (I have more than you)

Ik ben de beste speler. (I am the best player)

Om de wereld te veroveren moet je of heel knap of heel slim zijn! (Oam dŭ we-rŭlt tŭ ver-oa-vŭ-rŭn moot yŭ of hail knupp of hail slim sine!) - To conquer the world you must be either very pretty or very smart!

En... en wat ben jij dan? (En... en wot ben yiye dun?) - And... and what are you then?

Wil je daarmee zeggen dat ik niet mooi ben? (Will yŭ dahr-may zeĝ-ĝun dot ik neet moy ben?) - Are you saying that I am not pretty?

Uh... nee... jawel, hoor. (Uh... nay... ya-well, hoar.) - Uhm... no... yes, you are... really.

Dan is het goed. (Don is het ĝoot.) - Then it's okay.

Ik ben gewoon mooi. (Ik ben ĝŭ-woan moy.) - I am just pretty.

Chapter 7: Weather

Okay, enough with the grammar for a bit. Let's try some everyday conversation, like the topic everyone starts when they don't have anything else to say: The weather. Here are some simple phrases that will help you keep up the conversation when you have no clue what to tell or ask them. You can always start talking about the weather, right?

Unlike in English, where people say "It is raining/snowing, etc." the Dutch simply say, "It snows" or "It rains." Pretty easy, right? Here is a small list of what you can say.

Het	
	regent (ray-ĝŭnt) - it is raining
	sneeuwt (snaywt) - it is snowing
	is mooi weer (is moy weir) - the weather is nice
	stormt (stormt) - there is a storm
	hagelt (hah-ĝŭlt) - there is hail
	waait hard (waayt heart) - there is a strong wind
	is tien graden Celsius (is teen ĝrah-dŭn Cell-see-yus) - It's 10 degrees Celsius
	is bewolkt (is bŭ-wohlkt) - it is cloudy

Other helpful words:

de wind (wint) - wind
het weer (het weir) - the weather
de temperatuur (dŭ tem-pŭ-rah-ture) - the temperature
het weerbericht (het weir-bŭ-riĝt) - the weather report
de zon (dŭ zon) - the sun

de wolken (dŭ wool-kŭn) - the clouds
de lucht (dŭ lŭĝt) - de sky/the air (same word in Dutch)

Other expressions:

Lekker weertje, hè? (Leck-kŭr weir-tyŭ, he?) - The weather is nice, isn't it?
Het giet. (Het ĝeet.) - It is pouring rain.
Het is mooi weer. (Het is moy weir.) - The weather is lovely.
Het is rotweer. (Het is roat-weir.) - This weather is terrible.
Laten we naar buiten gaan. (Lah-tŭn wŭ nahr bow-tŭn ĝahn.) - Let's go outside.
Ik blijf liever binnen. (Ik blife lee-vŭr bin-nŭn.) - I would rather stay inside.
Het is te donker om naar buiten te gaan. (Het is tŭ don-kŭr oam nahr bow-tŭn tŭ ĝahn.) - It is too dark to go outside.

Chapter 8: Travel

When you are traveling, there are always some words and expressions that can be useful. In this chapter I will give you some of those so you can handle yourself.

By the way, the Dutch and Belgian airports have a lot of things explained in English on the signs. There is no need to worry that you have to ask for directions a lot.

Tulpen in de beroemde Keukenhof (tulips in the famous Keukenhof gardens)

Een molen (a windmill)

Amsterdam

Het Atonium (near Brussels)

Brugge (Belgium)

Useful Words

Toerist (tourist) - tourist

Reizen (rise-ŭn) - to travel

Fototoestel (photo-too-stell) - camera

Camera (kah-mŭ-rah) - camera

Kaart (kahrt) - map

Trein (trine) - train

Vliegtuig (fleeĝ-towĝ) - airplane

Vliegveld (fleeĝ-felt) - airport

Auto (ouw-tow) - car

Bus (bŭs) - bus

Taxi (tuck-see) - taxi

Hotel (hotel) - hotel

Meneer (mŭ-near) - Mr.

Mevrouw (mŭ-frow) - Mrs.

Overnachten (over-nuĝ-tŭn) - stay/spend the night

Koffer (kof-fŭr) - suitcase

Tas (tuss) - bag

Rugzak (rŭĝ-suck) - rucksack/backpack

Meenemen (may-nay-mŭn) - take with you

Kleren (clear-ŭn) - clothes

Spullen (spŭl-lŭn) - stuff/belongings

Douane (doo-ah-nŭ) - customs

Buitenland (bow-tŭn-lunt) - foreign country

Vakantie (fuck-cun-see [sorry, but that's how you say it]) - vacation

Zakenreis (sah-cŭn-rise) - business trip

Common Expressions

Ik ben op vakantie. (Ik ben oap fuck-cun-see.) - I am on vacation

Ik kom uit Amerika. (Ik comb out Ah-mear-ee-kha.) - I am from America.

Ik kom uit Engeland. (Ik comb out Ang-ŭ-lunt) - I am from England.

Ik blijf twee weken. (Ik blife tway way-kŭn) - I am staying for two weeks.

Waar moet ik heen? (Wahr moot ik hain?) - Where should I go?

Waar kan ik mijn koffer halen? (Wahr cun ik mine kof-fŭr hah-lŭn?) - Where can I get my suitcase?

Kunt u mij helpen? (Cŭnt ew my hel-pŭn?) - Can you help me?

Kunt u een foto van mij maken? (Cŭnt ew ŭn photo fun my mah-kŭn?) - Could you take a picture of me?

Ik kan een beetje Nederlands. (Ik cun ŭn bay-tyŭ Nay-dŭr-lunts) - I can speak a little Dutch.

Ik spreek Engels. (Ik sprayk Ang-ŭls.) - I speak English

Wat zegt u? (Wot seĝt ew?) - What did you say?

Geen idee. (ĝayn ee-day) - No idea.

Chapter 9: Relationships and Romance

Who am I to say you might not end up liking a pretty Dutch girl or handsome Dutch guy so much that you want get to know them more? Here are some expressions that make it more interesting for him or her, because you can speak in their native language and express your interest.

Wat doe je graag in je vrije tijd? (Wot do yŭ ĝrahĝ in yŭ vrye-yŭ tite?) - What do you like to do in your free time?

Waar kom je vandaan? (Wahr comb yŭ von-dahn?) - Where are you from?

Hoe heet je? (Who hate yŭ?) - What is your name?

Ik hou van je (Ik how fun yŭ) - I love you

Ik vind je lief (ik fint yŭ leef) - I think you're sweet

Je hebt mooie ogen (Yŭ hept moa-yŭ oa-ĝŭn) - You have beautiful eyes

Ik ben gek op je (Ik ben ĝeck op yŭ) - I am crazy about you

Wil je een relatie? (Will yŭ ŭn ray-lah-tsee?) - Do you want a relationship (with me)?

Wil je met me trouwen? (Will yŭ met mŭ trou-wŭn?) - Will you marry me?

Hoeveel ex-vriendinnen heb je? (Who-fail ex-freen-din-nŭn hep yŭ?) - How many ex-girlfriends do you have?

Hoeveel ex-vrienden heb je? (Who-fail ex-freen-dŭn hep yŭ?) - How many ex-boyfriends do you have?

Heb je morgen tijd? (Hep yŭ mor-ĝŭn tite?) - Do you have time tomorrow?

Hoeveel kinderen heb je? (Who-fail kin-dŭ-rŭn hep yŭ?) - How many kids do you have?

Heb je een relatie? (Hep yŭ ŭn ray-lah-tsee?) - Are you in a relationship/are you single?

Wil je iets leuks gaan doen? (Will yŭ eets leyks ĝahn doon?) - Do you want to do something fun?

Mooie jurk (Moy-yŭ yŭrk) - Nice dress

Je ziet er goed uit (Yŭ seat air leyk out) - You look good

Wat zoek je in een man/vrouw? (Wot sewk yŭ in ŭn mun/frow?) - What are you looking for in a man/woman?

Wat zit jij naar mijn dochter te kijken?

Why are you looking at my daughter? (Literally: What sit you at my daughter to look?)

Chapter 10: Diminutives

In English, sometimes putting the letter "-y" or "-ey" gets added to a word, especially in children's play or kindergarten, to make it smaller without using the word "little" or anything similar. A few examples: Horsey, bunny, doggie, etc.

It's not as common though, and it doesn't happen with every word. But in Dutch, you can make ANYTHING small by adding "-je" or "-etje" or "-tje" or "-pje" to it. It depends a little on the end vowel or consonant what it is and what's correct exactly, but just know that you can use it on a lot.

When a word ends at a vowel that should be pronounced long, like "auto," in the diminutive, the extra "-o" and the "-t" get added. If a word ends at an "-m," for instance, then it adds the letter "-p," like in "boompje." When the original word ends at an "l" or an "r," for example, the extra "-t" gets added, like in "kikkertje." And there are other ways to know, with its fair share of numerous exceptions.

See the following examples.

In all these cases below, the first word is the original, the second word means "little..." (with whatever the word is), and the third word is the translation

Bank - bankje - bank

Auto - autootje - car

Vis - visje - fish

Kikker - kikkertje - frog

Huis - huisje - house

Bal - balletje - ball

Bed - bedje - bed

Tafel - tafeltje - table

Jongen - jongetje - boy

Meisje (this word is always small; there is no "meis" at all) - girl

Muur - muurtje - wall

Vuur - vuurtje - fire

Plant - plantje - plant

Boom - boompje - tree

Bloem - bloempje - flower

Emmer - emmertje - bucket

Scherm - schermpje - screen

Bril - brilletje - glasses (singular in Dutch)

Sok - sokje - sock

Now that you got a lot to study and think about, I hope to see you in the next book so we can have more fun learning Dutch and go over some other topics. Download and study all three of these books and you'll be awesome at speaking Dutch!

Dan spreek je pas ECHT goed Nederlands! (Then you'll REALLY speak Dutch well!)

Thanks again for buying my book. If you have a minute, please leave a positive review. You can leave your review by clicking on this link:

Leave your review here. Thank you!

I take reviews seriously and always look at them. This way, you are helping me provide you better content that you will LOVE in the future. A review doesn't have to be long, just one or two sentences and a number of stars you find appropriate (hopefully 5 of course).

Also, if I think your review is useful, I will mark it as "helpful." This will help you become more known on Amazon as a decent reviewer, and will ensure that more authors will contact you with free e-books in the future. This is how we can help each other.

DISCLAIMER: This information is provided "as is." The author, publishers and/or marketers of this information disclaim any loss or liability, either directly or indirectly as a consequence of applying the information presented herein, or in regard to the use and application of said information. No guarantee is given, either expressed or implied, in regard to the merchantability, accuracy, or acceptability of the information. The pages within this e-book have been copyrighted.

Speak Dutch
Book 3 of 3: Advanced

By Vincent Noot

Copyright @2015

All rights reserved. No part of this book may be reproduced in any form or by any means without permission in writing from the publisher, Vincent Noot.

If you like my book, please leave a positive review on Amazon. I would appreciate it a lot. Thanks! This is the link:

Subscribe to my blog: lifechangingebooksblog.blogspot.com

You can also visit my Facebook page.

Or you can look at my Pinterest board.

Contents:

Introduction	156
Chapter 1: False Friends	158
Chapter 2: Proverbs	161
Chapter 3: Puns	163
Chapter 4: Inversion	168
Chapter 5: Conversation	176
Chapter 6: Customs	180
Chapter 7: Health	187
Chapter 8: Countries and Languages	189

Introduction

This book is for those who have read the first two books or for people who are familiar with the Dutch language, but want to learn some more advanced ways of saying things, some common pitfalls they might have overlooked, and are excited to perfect their Dutch language skills even more.

For those who haven't bought the first or second book, let me tell you something about myself. As you might have seen from my last name (and yes, that's my actual name), I am of Dutch origin. In fact, I grew up in the Netherlands. My native language is Dutch, but over the years, as I have lived in several English speaking countries and interacted with many foreigners, I have mastered that language as well. I now speak both languages fluently to the point where most people can't even hear my Dutch accent anymore.

In the past, I have worked for a translation office (English to Dutch), and have become precise and exact at translating, correcting, reviewing, and proofing documents in both Dutch and English. Because of my experience in translation work and numerous editing jobs, and with my cultural background, I am confident to say that I will be one of the best Dutch language teachers you'll find. I will show you how to learn and master the Dutch language.

Languages don't have to be hard. It's all about understanding the structure of a language, not just memorizing thousands of words. Memorizing a dictionary will, however useful, only get you so far. Forming sentences and understanding grammar, the logic, and structure of a language is a whole study. One can only speak a language fluently by being completely imbedded in it for years. But at least with these 3 books, I can teach you the most important basics, and get you going, so that you'll be more confident in speaking up and reading or writing Dutch.

The ebook version of this book has a link to a BONUS video in chapter 5. Check it out by downloading it!

Common mistakes many native English speakers make when they attempt to speak Dutch, is copy an English proverb that doesn't make any sense in Dutch, false friends (words that look alike, but mean something completely different), or failing to use inversion (turning around the verbs and other words correctly). These are more ways to master the Dutch language and sound like you know what you are talking about. By studying this 3rd book, you'll notice that people who speak Dutch can relate better and understand what you are saying. Did I spark your curiosity yet? Wacht dan niet langer en ga verder! (Then don't wait any longer and continue!)

Chapter 1: False Friends

An "Anglicism" is a word, sentence or phrase that comes from English but does not go along with the correct form in the language it is translated into. With words, they are often called "false friends." Here are some common examples:

The word "alarm" could refer to the Dutch alarm, but it could also mean "wekker" which is, more accurately, an alarm clock that helps you wake up.

Other expressions:

English
Best Translation   Mistake

English	Best Translation	Mistake
Stop the ball!	Stop de bal!	Houd de bal tegen!
Serious pain	Serieuze pijn	Ernstige pijn
Under construction	Onder constructie	In aanbouw
Sooner or later	Vroeger of later	Vroeg of laat
The book says...	Het boek zegt...	In het boek staat...
Apply to your life	Op je leven toepassen	Op jezelf toepassen
A direct conncetion	Een directe connectie	Een rechtstreekse verbinding
Dramatic changes	Dramatische veranderingen	Drastische veranderingen

In the same way, there are Dutch phrases and words you think you might recognize, but they are deceivingly different in their meanings. Check out the following example:

Eekhoorn

Dutch	English assumption	Best English Translation
Een brave man	A brave man	A harmless man

Hij is in de war	He is in the war	He is confused
Actueel	Actual	Current/nowadays
Eekhoorn	Acorn	Squirrel (an "acorn" is een "eikel" in Dutch)
Magazijn	Magazine	Warehouse
Raar	Rare	Weird/strange
Mening	Meaning	Opinion
Invalide	Invalid	Handicapped
Map	Map	Folder/binder
File	File	Traffic jam
Advocaat	Advocate	Lawyer
Eventueel	Eventually	By chance
Spel	Spell	Game

Another common mistake, like I mentioned in one of the previous books, is thinking that the Dutch call you a "whore" when they say, "Dat is goed, hoor." It is just an emphasis, nothing more. Oh, and don't think the Dutch have any bad intentions when they say "douchen," (doo-shen). It just means taking a shower, similar to the Spanish "duchar."

Chapter 2: Proverbs

One of my family members who had lived in the United States for a long time cracked me up on accident when she said, "Er is iets vissigs aan de hand" (There is something fishy going on.) Why? Because that proverb simply doesn't exist in Dutch. We all knew what she meant, but it was hilarious, since she didn't make the switch. I have heard other visitors from America say things like, "Dat is een stukje gebak" (That is a piece of cake.) No, it didn't make any sense to those who didn't know enough English.

So on that funny note, I will give you some common Dutch proverbs, with their pronunciation, translation, and meaning.

Oude koeien uit de sloot halen (Ouw-dŭ coo-yŭ out dŭ slowt hah-lŭn) - Getting old cows out of the mote - Bringing up something that should be left in the past (like the time you broke your mother-in-law's best plates ten years ago)

Door het lint gaan (Door het lint ĝahn) - Going through the ribbon - Not being able to control your anger or emotions (like that time that Windows was shutting down for no reason and you didn't press "save")

Ik heb er kaas van gegeten (Ik hep air kahs fun ĝŭ-ĝay-tŭn) - I have eaten cheese from it - I know everything about it (like you will about Dutch after you read this book series)

Hij neemt de benen (Hye naimt dŭ bay-nŭn) - He takes the legs - He is getting out of here/there (like when your toilet exploded and you had to avoid the smell by sleeping at your neighbor's place)

Een fluitje van een cent (ŭn flouw-tyŭ fun ŭn cent) - A flute of a cent - a piece of cake/very easy (like mastering the Dutch language)

Wat de boer niet kent, dat vreet hij niet (Wot dŭ boor neet kent, dot vrayt hye neet) - What the farmer doesn't know, he doesn't eat - Not being willing to try out new things (like when your wife asked you to wear something pink and purple for tonight's dinner)

Boontje komt om zijn loontje (Bown-tyŭ komt oam zine lown-tyŭ) - Bean comes around his bean - He/she gets what he/she deserves (like that bad grade you got when you were partying instead of studying in the weekend)

Vele handen maken licht werk (Vay-lŭ hun-dŭn mah-kŭn liĝt wairk) - Many hands make light work - If more people help out, the job will be done faster (like that time a few people from the church helped you move)

Blaffende honde bijten niet (Bluf-fŭn-dŭ hoan-dŭn bite-ŭn neet) - Barking dogs don't bite - Someone who threatens you, might not always be an immediate danger

Praatjes vullen geen gaatjes (prah-tyŭs vŭl-lŭn ĝain ĝah-tyŭs) - Chats don't fill holes - Talk is cheap (like that guy your uncle tried to convince you that it would be good for you to perform free labor for him)

Een ongeluk zit in een klein hoekje (ŭn on-ĝŭ-lŭck zit in ŭn kline hoo-kyŭ) - An accident is in a little corner - Accidents are waiting to happen/there isn't much needed for an accident (like when someone lifts up the bed too high and breaks the light on the ceiling [based on a true story])

Als de kat van huis is, springen de muizen op tafel (Uls dŭ cut fun house is, spring-ŭn dŭ mouse-ŭn oap tah-fŭl) - When the cat leaves the house, the mice jump on the table - When an authority figure leaves, chaos breaks loose and control is gone (like that time you came home and your kids messed up the living room)

Chapter 3: Puns

If you want to sound funny or smart, or be a little social by telling "woordgrappen" (word jokes, or in other words: Puns), then I have some good ones for you. These are jokes that will mostly only work in Dutch, which is why it will be beneficial to know the language.

Sentences and Jokes

Ken je die mop van die mummie? Ingewikkeld, hè? (Ken yŭ dee mop fun dee mŭm-mee? In-ĝŭ-wick-ckŭlt, hea?) - Do you the joke of that mummy? Complicated, isn't it?

The reason why this is funny, is because the word "inwikkelen" or in other words, the past participle "ingewikkeld" means "enwrapped" or "enveloped" or "enrolled." But it has a double meaning, since it also means, "complicated."

Ik wil stemmen, maar ik heb geen ID/idee (Ik will stem-mŭn, mahr ik hep ĝain ee-day) - I want to vote, but I have no ID.

The reason why this is funny, and it would probably work in English too, is that the word "ID" is pronounced the same way as "idea." So he has no idea how to vote, but he also has no ID to vote.

Het ene ei zegt tegen het andere ei: 'Niet zo dicht bij de rand komen.' Het andere ei antwoordt: 'Ach, klets!' (Het aye-nŭ eye zeĝt tay-ĝŭn het un-dŭ-rŭ eye, "Neet so diĝt by dŭ runt koa-mŭn." Het un-dŭ-rŭ eye unt-war-t, "Aĝ, klets!") - The one egg says to the other egg, "Don't go too close to the edge." The other egg answers, "Oh, nonsense!"

This is funny because the word "Klets" means to chat or speak nonsense, but at the same time, it can be a sound effect of a broken egg. So the egg is saying it is nonsense to be so cautious, but is falling down at the same time and breaking on the floor.

Wauw! Dat moet wel een grote vis zijn! (Wow! That must be a big fish!)

Ja! Help je nog mee of hoe zit het? (Yes! Are you going to help me or what?)

Waaah! Help! (Waaah! Help!)

Zou het daarom een 'werphengel' heten? (Is that why it is called a "fishing rod"?

Plons! (Splash!)

Explanation: "werpen" means "to throw" and "hengel" is rod. In this case, however, the main character is not throwing the rod, but is being thrown by the rod.

Fruit and Vegetable Jokes

These are guessing jokes. You say, "Het... en.... Wat is het?" In other words, you give them a couple of clues and then let them guess what it is. If they don't know within 3 seconds, you give them the answer and make them laugh. Especially kids will love these jokes.

Het is groen en skiet door de bergen. Wat is het? (Het is ĝroon en skeet door dŭ ber-ĝŭn. Wot is het?) - It is green and skis through the mountains. What is it?

Een skiwi (ŭn skee-wee) - a ski-kiwi.

Het is groen en hangt onder de auto. Wat is het? (Het is ĝroon en hungt oan-dŭr dŭ ow-tow. Wot is het?) - It is green and is hanging under the car. What is it?

Een spruitlaat (ŭn sprout-laht) - a Brussel sprouts exhaust (spruit uitlaat)

Het is groen en je kunt ermee rijden. Wat is het? (Het is ĝroon en yŭ kŭnt air-may ride-ŭn. Wot is het?) - It is green and you can drive with it. What is it?

Een preibewijs (ŭn prye-bŭ-wise) - A leek driver's license (prei rijbewijs)

Het is geel en je hangt het aan de auto. Wat is het? (Het is ĝail en yŭ hungt het ahn dŭ ow-tow. Wot is het?) - It is yellow and you can hang it on the car. What is it?

Een banaanhangwagen (ŭn ba-nahn-hung-wah-ĝŭn) - A banana trailer (banaan aanhangwagen)

Het is rood en heeft een baard. Wat is het? (Het is rowt en hayft ŭn bahrt. Wot is het?) - It is red and it has a beard. What is it?

Een baardbei (ŭn bahrt-bye) - a beard strawberry (baard aardbei)

Het is groen en het drijft. Wat is het? (Het is ĝroon en het drife-t. Wot is het?) - It is green and it floats. What is it.

Andrijvie (On-drive-ee) - floating andive (drijf andijvie)

Chapter 4: Inversion

All right, enough joking around. Let's get serious. Let's do some hardcore, tough GRAMMAR! In this chapter, you'll learn about one of the most annoying things for people who are native English speakers, something they do both in Dutch and in German, but for some reason the English never got around to it: Inversion.

It is something I have seen one American after another struggle that came to the Netherlands or Belgium. Even though they studied the language for months, they still didn't get it right. It takes a moment to pause for beginners and think about how to put the right words into the right order. For someone who is already used to being around more Dutch people for a longer period of time, I think they should be able to pick it up after a while.

When I studied languages like French, Spanish, and Thai, I noticed that the order in which you put the words makes all the difference. It distinguishes people who speak it fluently or more perfectly from those who are struggling to get something out of their mouths. If you keep making mistakes with this though, don't be too hard on yourself. Be happy to accept corrections, think about it, and move on. People who learn a language the fastest, are those who keep trying and aren't embarrassed to make mistakes (that is exactly why children pick it up so quickly... they are often humble enough to parrot what everybody else says and aren't afraid to make mistakes).

What is inversion? Inversion simply means to invert (switch places) words in the sentence that otherwise would be in a different order. I will show you when the Dutch (and often the Germans) use inversion.

Inversion often happens when the subject is NOT at the beginning of a sentence anymore, or in case of most clauses. This is usually the case with conjunctions or times mentioned as the first word of the sentence.

In a regular sentence, the verb and subject get switched.

When this happens (in a clause) with a conjunction (like "because" or "when" or "since"), the main verb in that sentence gets pushed all the way to the end of the sentence and appears as the last word.

Here are some examples. Hopefully these will help you understand what is going on.

Regular sentences

Ik ga naar huis. (Ik ĝah nahr house.) - I am going home.

Morgen ga ik naar huis. (Moar-ĝŭn ĝah ik nahr house.) - Tomorrow I will go home.

See how "ga" (go) and "ik" (I) get turned around?

Ik was heel blij. (Ik was hail blye.) - I was very happy.

Gisteren was ik heel bij. (ĝis-tŭ-rŭn was ik hail blye.) - Yesterday I was very happy.

Same principle. Here "was" and "ik" get turned around because the time is mentioned first.

Sentences with Conjunctions

Just to make it harder on you... (ughh... sorry... I did not invent the language) SOME conjunctions are followed by inversion and some others are NOT. Here is a list of some of the most important conjunctions and a yes or no about whether or not they are followed by inversion. In the cases I filled out "yes" the verb gets shoved all the way to the back. There are a few exceptions where the subject and verb get switched. When that is the case, I have indicated so.

A little side note: If the conjunction appears in the clause, in the first part of the sentence, it switches around the subject and verb of the second part of the sentence in many cases. When this is the case with a conjugation, I will show it through examples. Yes, I know... it's complicated, but hopefully the following overview will help, as well as the examples I am going to give you.

Want (because) - no

Maar (but) - no

En (and) - no

Hoewel (although) - yes

Als (if/when) - yes

Terwijl (while) - yes

Omdat (because) - yes

Zodat (so that) - yes

Totdat (until) - yes

Dus (so/thus) - switched

Daarom (therefore) - switched

I will now give you an example with every conjunction, just so you understand the concept better.

Want

Ik ben moe. Ik heb de hele dag gewerkt. (Ik ben moo. Ik hep dŭ hay-lŭ duĝ ĝŭ-wairkt.) - I am tired. I worked all day.

Ik ben moe, want ik heb de hele dag gewerkt. (Ik ben moo, wunt ik hep dŭ hay-lŭ duĝ ĝŭ-wairkt.) - I am tired, because I worked all day.

Easy, right? Since the word "want" is not followed by inversion, you can just connect the sentences and you're done. So if you're iffy about using inversion, I recommend you to always use "want" instead of "omdat." It's just easier that way, because you don't have to mix everything up.

Maar

Ik moet naar school. Ik heb geen zin. (Ik moot nahr sĝohl. Ik hep ĝain zin.) - I have to go to school. I don't feel like going.

Ik moet naar school, maar ik heb geen zin. (Ik moot nahr sĝohl, mahr ik hep ĝain zin.) - I have to go to school, but I don't feel like going.

The word "maar" in Dutch is easy. No inversion.

En

Ik moet weg. Ik heb haast. (Ik moot weĝ. Ik hep hahst.) - I have to go. I am in a hurry.

Ik moet weg en ik heb haast. (Ik moot weĝ en ik hep hahst.) - I have to go and I am in a hurry.

Easy. No inversion

Hoewel

Ik ben te laat. Ik doe rustig aan. (Ik ben tŭ laht. Ik doo rŭs-tiĝ ahn.) - I am too late. I am taking it easy.

Hoewel ik te laat ben, doe ik het rustig aan. (Who-well ik tŭ laht ben, doo ik het rŭs-tiĝ ahn.) - Although I am too late, I am taking it easy.

Because the word "hoewel" appears in the first part of the sentence, the word "doe" and "ik" get switched around in the second part of the sentence.

Ik doe het rustig aan, hoewel ik te laat ben. (Ik doo het rŭs-tiĝ ahn, who-well ik tŭ laht ben.) - I am taking it easy, although I am too late.

Because the word "hoewel" appears in the SECOND part of the sentence, the word "ben" (am) gets pushed all the way to the back.

Als

Je bent weg. Ik ga feesten. (Yŭ ĝaht weĝ. Ik ĝah fay-stŭn.) - You are gone/away. I am going to party.

Als je weg bent, ga ik feesten. (Oals yŭ weĝ bent, ĝah ik fay-stŭn.) - If/when you are gone, I am going to party.

Because the word "als" appears in the first part of the sentence, the words "ga" and "ik" get turned around in the second part of the sentence. Also, the word "bent" get's pushed to the end of the first part of the sentence as part of the inversion.

Ik ga feesten als je weg bent. (Ik ĝah fay-stŭn oals yŭ weĝ bent.) - I am going to party if/when you are gone.

Here inversion only applies to the second part of the sentence, where "bent" gets pushed to the back. The first part of the sentence is FREE and stays the same.

Terwijl

Je was in de auto. Je luisterde naar de radio. (Yŭ was in de ow-tow. Yŭ lou-stŭr-dŭ nahr dŭ rah-dee-o.) - You were in the car. You were listening to the radio.

Je luisterde naar de radio terwijl je in de auto was. (Yŭ lou-stŭr-dŭ nahr dŭ rah-dee-o tare-well yŭ in dŭ ow-tow was.) - You were listening to the radio while you were in the car.

The first part of the sentence stays the same, but in the second part, the word "was" gets pushed towards the back.

Terwijl je in de auto was, luisterde je naar de radio. (Tare-well yŭ in dŭ ow-tow was, lou-stŭr-dŭ yŭ nahr dŭ rah-dee-o.) - While you were in the car, you were listening to the radio.

Here the conjunction appears as the first word of the sentence, so in the first part of the sentence, the verb "was" goes towards the back of that sentence, and in the second part the words "je" and "luisterde" get turned around.

Omdat

Ik doe mijn jas aan. Ik heb het koud. (Ik doo mine yus ahn. Ik hep het cowt.) - I am putting on my jacket. I am cold.

Ik doe mijn jas aan, omdat ik het koud heb. (Ik doo mine yus ahn, oam-dot Ik het cowt hep.) - I am putting on my jacket, because I am cold.

The word "omdat" appears in the second part of the sentence, so the word "heb" gets pushed towards the back. There are sentences that start with "omdat" but they are less common.

Zodat

Ik leer hard voor mijn toets, zodat ik een goed cijfer krijg. (Ik lere heart four mine toots, so-dot ik ŭn ĝoot cipher kriĝe.) - I am studying hard for my test, so that I will get a good grade.

The word "krijg" means "get," but because of the inversion dependent on "zodat," it gets pushed all the way to the back of the sentence.

Totdat

Je mag tv kijken totdat je naar bed moet. (Yŭ moĝ tay-vay kye-ckŭn toat-dot yŭ nahr bet moot.) - You may watch TV until you must go to bed.

The word "moet" gets shoved towards the back because of the conjunction "totdat."

Dus

Ik heb vandaag veel geld, dus ben ik in een goed humeur. (Ik hep von-dahĝ vail ĝelt, dŭs ben ik in ŭn ĝoot hew-mŭr.) - I have lots of money today, so I am in a good mood.

The words "ben" and "ik" got turned around. Usually it's "ik ben" but because of "dus," they switched places. A little side note: Sometimes when talking fast, the Dutch don't turn them around and it can still be somewhat correct. They could say, "...dus ik ben in een goed humeur" and get away with it.

Daarom

De zon schijnt. Daarom ga ik naar buiten. (Dŭ zon sĝine-t. Dah-rom ĝah ik nahr bow-tŭn.) - De sun in shining. Therefore, I am going outside.

Normally it would be "ik ga naar buiten" but because of the word "Daarom" at the beginning of the sentence, it is "ga ik" instead of "ik ga."

Chapter 5: Conversation

Grammar... grammar... grammar... enough of that now. Let's start with some everyday conversations that you could learn to talk to other Dutch-speaking people.

One of the best ways to start speaking a language faster is LOTS and LOTS of conversation. Just start speaking to others and figuring it out. That is one of the best way to perfect it, pick up the pronunciation, and learn faster and easier.

Just to help you with pronunciation, if you downloaded the E-book, you can look at the YouTube video to hear me pronounce the words in these conversations.

Click HERE for the YouTube Video!

Hoi, ik heet Erik. Hoe heet jij? (Hoy, ik hate Ere-ik. Who hate yeye?) - Hi, my name is Eric. What is yours?	**Ik heet Marieke. Hoe lang ben je hier al?** (Ik hate Mah-ree-kŭ. Who long ben yŭ here all? - My name is Marieke. How long have you been here?
Nog maar een half uur. Zullen we naar binnen gaan? (Noĝ mahr ŭn hulf ure. Zŭl-lŭn wŭ nahr bin-nŭn ĝahn.) - Only for a half hour. Shall we go inside?	**Ja, is goed.** (Yah, is ĝoot.) - Yes. All right.
Dus hoe oud ben je? (Dŭs who owt ben yŭ?) - So how old are you?	**Ik ben vijfentwintig. En jij?** (Ik ben vife-en-twin-tiĝ. En yeye?) - I am twenty-five. And you?
Ik ben achtentwintig. Wat voor werk doe je? (Ik ben aĝt-en-twin-tiĝ. Wot four wairk doo yŭ?) - I am twenty-	**Eigenlijk studeer ik.** (Eye-ĝŭn-lŭk stew-dear ik.) - Actually, I am in college.

eight. What kind of work do you do?	
O, leuk. Wat dan? (Oh, leyk. Wot done?) - Oh, fun. What is your major?	**Ik studeer geneeskunde.** (Ik stew-dear ĝŭ-nays-kŭn-dŭ.) - I am in medical school.
Interessant. Mijn vader is arts. (In-tŭ-rŭ-sunt. Mine fah-dŭr is arts.) - Interesting. My father is a doctor.	**Wauw! Wat een toeval. Wat doe jij?** (Wow! Wot ŭn too-fall. Wot doo yeye?) - Wow! What a coincidence. What do you do?
Ik werk in de bouw, maar ik ben op zoek naar een andere baan. (Ik wairk in dŭ bow, mahr ik ben op sook nahr ŭn un-dŭ-rŭ bahn.) - I am in construction, but I am looking for another job.	**Wat wil je dan gaan doen?** (Wot will yŭ done ĝahn doon?) - What do you want to do then?
Ik wil graag manager worden, dus ga ik terug naar school. (Ik will ĝrahĝ manager woar-dŭn, dŭs ĝah ik trŭĝ nahr sĝoal.) - I want to become a manager, so I am going back to school.	**Geweldig. Dat lijkt me een goed plan.** (ĝŭ-well-diĝ. Dot like-t mŭ ŭn ĝoot plun.) - Great. That seems like a good plan to me.

Schatje, ik ga boodschappen doen. (Sĝot-yŭ, ik ĝah boat-sĝop-pŭn doon.) - Honey, I am going grocery shopping.	**Wacht even!** (Wuĝt aye-fŭn!) - Wait a minute!
Wat is er dan? (Wot is air done?) - What is going on?	**Ik heb nog wat dingen van de supermarkt nodig.** (Ik hep noĝ wut dingŭn fun dŭ sew-pŭr-markt no-dŭĝ.) - I still need some things from the supermarket.
O... nou ik ga maar even, hoor. (Oh... now, ik ĝah mahr	**Kun je dan wat rijst meenemen?** (Kŭn yŭ done

aye-fŭn, hoar.) - Oh, well, I am just out for a minute really.	wot rice-t may-nay-mŭn?) - Can you get some rice then?
Vooruit dan maar. (Four-out done mahr.) - Okay, all right then.	**Dankjewel. Dat scheelt me enorm veel tijd.** (Dunk-yŭ-well. Dot sĝailt mŭ ay-norm vail tite.) - Thank you. That will save me an enormous amount of time.
Goed. Tot straks. (ĝoot. Tot strucks.) - Okay, see you later!	**Ja, doei!** (Yah, dooy!) - Yes. Goodbye!

Kunt u mij vertellen waar het treinstation is? (Kŭnt ew my fair-tell-ŭn wahr het trine-stah-shun is?) - Can you tell me where the trainstation is?	**Het is best dichtbij.** (Het is best diĝt-bye.) - It is pretty close.
Ja? Mooi zo. (Yah? Moy so.) - Yeah? Oh, good.	**Luister goed. Eerst ga je rechtsaf. Dan linksaf. Daarna rechtdoor, en dan zie je het aan de rechterkant.** (Low-stŭr ĝoot. Ere-st ĝah yŭ lings-off. Dahr-nah reĝt-door, en done see yŭ het ahn dŭ reĝ-tŭr-cunt.) - Listen carefully. First you turn right. Then left. After that you go straight, and then you will see it on the right side.
Aha. Dat klinkt makkelijk. (Aha. Dot klinkt muck-kŭ-lŭck.) - Aha. That sounds easy.	**Ja, je bent er binnen een paar minuten.** (Yah, yŭ bent air bin-nŭn ŭn pahr mi-new-tŭn.) - Yes, you will be there within a few minutes.
Bedankt. Ik ga meteen. Tot	**Graag gedaan. Succes!**

ziens! (Bŭ-dunkt. Ik ĝah mŭ-tain.) - Thanks. I will go right away.	(ĝrahĝ ĝŭ-dahn. Seucksess!) - You're welcome. Good luck!

Zullen we deze film kijken? (Zŭl-lŭn wŭ day-sŭ film kye-ckŭn?) - Shall we watch this movie?	Welke? (Well-kŭ?) - Which one?
Die actiefilm met Tom Cruise. (Dee uck-see-film met Tom Cruise.) - That action movie with Tom Cruise.	Ik kijk liever naar een romantische komedie. (Ik kyke lee-fur nahr ŭn roam-un-tee-sŭ ko-may-dee.) - I would rather watch a romantic comedy.
Echt waar? Nou, ik vind zulke films maar saai. (Eĝt wahr? Now, ik fint zŭl-kŭ films mahr siye.) - Really? Well, I think those kinds of movies are boring.	Alsjeblieft? (Uls-yŭ-bleeft?) - Please?
Goed. Eerst kijken we naar een romantische film en daarna naar een actiefilm. (ĝoot. Ere-st ky-kŭn wŭ nahr ŭn roam-un-tee-sŭ film en dahr-nah nahr ŭn uck-see-film.) - Okay. First we will watch a romantic movie and then an action movie.	Afgesproken. (Off-ĝŭ-sproa-ckŭn.) - Agreed.
Kun jij de chips uit de keuken halen? (Kŭn yeye dŭ ships out dŭ cew-cŭn hah-lŭn?) - Can you get the chips from the kitchen?	Ja, zet jij intussen de film aan? (Yah, zet yeye in-tŭs-sŭn dŭ film ahn?) - Yes, will you turn on the movie in the meantime?
Natuurlijk. (Nah-ture-lŭck.) - Of course.	

Chapter 6: Customs

If you happen to go to the Netherlands, just keep in mind that not only the language is a little different, but the culture as well. Here are some things to take into account.

Offering a drink

Usually when you enter someone's home, one of the first things they do is asking, "Wil je iets drinken?" The Dutch have a strong tradition of offering visitors a drink, so expect it and if you want to be polite, do it when others enter your home too.

Saying what you think/speaking your mind

Of course there are exceptions, as is the case with every country with millions of people, but in a general sense, the Dutch are very forward and often speak their minds. That has pros and cons. A benefit could be that you know they're usually not hiding their feelings from you and they are often "honest" about what they think. They often say what they mean. No guessing games. The downside can be that some people don't think before they speak, and therefore insult or offend some others. It can be pretty annoying if people express their opinion when you don't ask for it. So it's up to you if you like that culture. The Belgians, however, in a general sense, do that a lot less. They are often more "polite" but not always open about their feelings. Of course there are exceptions there too, like a couple of families I knew when I lived there who never backed off and said what they were thinking.

Be normal

The Dutch often use a common phrase like, "Doe normaal, man!" or "Doe eens [even] normaal!" (Act normal!) They expect a certain decent behavior and common sense from every person. If you are out of line or deviate from the normal way of doing things, you could hear that remark.

Taxes

The taxes are high, and the government support is high too in areas of education, welfare, health care, road construction, etc. If you are used to a more capitalized way of thinking, don't be shocked when you hear of the more socialistic approach of "the strong shoulders need to carry the load of the weak." Not that it is in any way close to communism, but the balance is there in a different way. Less opportunity maybe, but also less risk and more financial safety for every citizen. This aspect of their culture reflects a way of thinking that I will explain in the next point.

Equality

The Dutch have an equality mindset. The following are not my opinion per se, but just things you will find in the Dutch culture. This means that:

1 Taxes are higher and welfare too. So income differences are not as extreme as in some other capitalist countries. Not as many extremely rich billionaires or people on the street who have nowhere to go (the ones on the streets are often but not always drug addicts.)

2 There are lots of commercials and advertisements promoting charity organizations like "Warchild" and "Unicef" and some other global non-profit institutions. Why? Because the Dutch culture is that they care. They cannot stand the inequality in the world, so they want to help.

3 Many Dutch promote gay rights. This is also a phenomenon of having "the same rights" mindset.

4 Education is cheap. The government supports it and prevents schools from charging ridiculous tuition fees. Therefore, almost anyone can afford a higher education.

5 Many women work, as part of the sexual revolution that began in the 1970s. They speak up and consider themselves equal to men. Many households have double incomes.

6 There is a minimum wage for every job. Unions are strong, people cannot always be fired or quit immediately because of contract, laws, and agreements, and you don't have to worry about tipping too much at restaurants. The waiters and waitresses all get a minimum wage.

7 Dutch speak their minds, so they complain more than in some other cultures. They consider themselves having "rights."

Here is a joke that explains it all:

An American, a Scottish person, and a Dutch person are in a car. The car crashes. All three die suddenly. At the gate, St. Peter (no offense, it's just a joke) mentions that "this is a mistake. There is too much paperwork involved. But I will cut you some slack and give you a deal. If you give me 100 dollars right now, I will put you back in life without any harm." The American gets his wallet and says, "Deal!" He appears back at the spot and gets interviewed by others around him. "Where are the Scottish and the Dutch guy?" they ask. "Well," the American responds, "The Scottish person thought it was too expensive and the Dutch guy complained because he insisted that the government should be paying for him."

Eating out less

There is not as much eating out as, for instance, in the United States. Sometimes Dutch people go to a "snackbar" that sell French fries, sausages, and some other fast food, but in general, they cook at home more often.

Public transportation

Because gas is expensive, cars are expensive, driver's license are expensive, and car insurance is expensive.... well, you saw this coming... driving a car is expensive. That's why a lot of Dutch (and Belgians) take trains and busses everywhere. It is common and often crowded around rush hour. There is an amazing network of public transportation connections, so depending on where you're going, you might easily get there without a car.

Bicycles

Another thing the infrastructure does almost perfectly, is bicycle trails, signs, and facilities. You'll see thousands of bicycles in the Netherlands. I grew up riding my bike to work, school, shopping centers, etc.

History

The European countries have a history that dates back to World War II, the Dark Ages and even to the Roman Empire. If you like history, it will be interesting to see all the buildings, art, religions, statues, and stories.

Techno music

Despite its rich culture and history, and the variety of interests in those modern societies, there is a general trend in the Netherlands (and also in Germany, Austria, and some surrounding countries) of Techno, House, Hardcore, Rave, Dance, or Trance music. You'll find those fast beats a lot at night clubs and those countries offer some of the best Techno DJs in the world.

Soccer/football

The one time that the Dutch feel patriotic, besides the national celebration of the royal courts, is during the World Cup or Euro Cup. You'll see flags and colors everywhere, and during the game, there are hardly any cars on the road. During the rest of the year, soccer/football is a common and popular sport, especially for boys and men. The Dutch soccer/football team has, despite its tiny country size, often made it to the world finals or won impressive awards for its performance.

Chapter 7: Health

Here are some words and sentences you could use when you go to the doctor or talk with someone about your health problems.

Ik ben verkouden. (Ik ben fair-cow-dŭn.) - I have a cold.

Ik ben ziek. (Ik ben zeek.) - I am sick/ill.

Ik ben misselijk. (Ik ben miss-ŭ-lŭck.) - I feel nauseous.

Ik heb koorts. (Ik hep core-ts.) - I have a fever.

Ik heb griep. (Ik hep ĝreep.) - I have the flu.

Waar kan ik een dokter vinden? (Wahr cun ik ŭn dok-tŭr fin-dŭn?) - Where can I find a doctor?

Waar is het ziekenhuis? (Wahr is het see-ckŭn-house?) - Where is the hospital? (Literally: Where is the sick house?)

Ik heb een pil nodig. (Ik hep ŭn pill no-dŭĝ.) - I need a pill.

Waar zijn mijn medicijnen? (Wahr sine mine may-dee-sine-nŭn?) - Where is my medicine?

Het doet hier pijn. (Het doot heer pine.) - It hurts here. (Literally: It does here pain.)

Het is niet ernstig. (Het is neet air-n-stŭĝ.) - It is not serious/nothing to worry about.

Ik heb een knie-operatie gehad. (Ik hep ŭn knee [pronounce the "k"]- o-pŭ-rah-tsee ĝŭ-hut.) - I had knee surgery.

Ik ben allergisch voor... (Ik ben ah-lair-ĝees four...) - I am allergic to...

Ik heb hoofdpijn. (Ik hep hoaft-pine.) - I have a headache.

Chapter 8: Countries and Languages

In this chapter, I will show you how to say a lot of different nationalities, languages, and countries in Dutch. Just so you know: The nationality and language is the same. So if you would say, "Hij spreekt Nederlands" (He speaks Dutch), it is the same for, "Hij is Nederlands" (He is Dutch), just like in English.

Nederland/Nederlands (Nay-dŭr-lunt/Nay-dŭr-lunts) - Netherlands/Dutch

Duitsland/Duits (Dowts-lunt/Dowts) - Germany/German

België/Vlaams/Frans (Bell-ĝee-yŭ/Vlahms/Fruns) - Belgium/Flemish/French

Frankrijk/Frans (Frunk-rike/Fruns) - France/French

Amerika/Amerikaans (Ah-mere-ee-ckah/Ah-mere-ee-ckahns) - America/American

Verenigde Staten (Fair-aye-nŭĝ-dŭ Stah-tŭn) - United States

Polen/Pools (Pow-lŭn/Powls) - Poland/Polish

Denemarken/Deens (Day-nŭ-mar-kŭn/Dayns) - Denmark/Danish

Engeland/Engels (Ang-ŭ-lunt/Ang-ŭls) - England/English

Schotland/Schots (Sĝot-lunt/Sĝots) - Scotland/Scottish

Ierland/Iers (Ere-lunt/Eres) - Ireland/Irish

Spanje/Spaans (Spun-yŭ/Spahns) - Spain/Spanish

Portugal/Portugees (Pore-too-ĝull/Pore-too-ĝays) - Portugal/Portuguese

China/Chinees (She-nah/She-nays) - China/Chinese

Japan/Japans (Yu-pun/Yu-puns) - Japan/Japanese

Mexico/Mexicaans (Mex-ee-co/Mex-ee/cahns) - Mexico/Mexican

Canada/Canadees (Cah-nah-dah/Cah-nah-days) - Canada/Canadian

Afrika/Afrikaans (Ah-free-cah/Ah-free-cahns) - Africa/African

Italië/Italiaans (Ee-tah-lee-yŭ/Ee-tah-lee-yahns) - Italy/Italian

Griekenland/Grieks (ĝree-ckŭn-lunt/ĝreecks) - Greece/Greek

Turkije/Turks (Tŭr-kye-yŭ/Tŭrks) - Turkey/Turkish

Noorwegen/Noors (Nore-way-ĝŭn/Nores) - Norway/Norwegian

Zweden/Zweeds (Sway-dŭn/Swayts) - Sweden/Swedish

Rusland/Russisch (Rŭs-lunt/Rŭs-sees) - Russia/Russian

Brazilië/Braziliaans (Brah-see-lee-yŭ/Bra-see-lee-yahns) - Brazil/Brazilian

In de Bijbel probeerde men een toren naar de hemel te bouwen - In the Bible, people tried to build a tower to Heaven.

[Speaking Thai] - Mae kowjai. - I don't understand.

[Speaking Spanish] Que es eso? - What is that?

[Speaking German] Ich weiß nicht was du sagst. - I don't know what you're saying.

[Speaking French] Je ne comprend pas. - I don't understand.

Well, I hope you had some fun with this. I hope you got a lot better at Dutch. Remember to have fun and try to get a feeling for the language, not just to bash endless vocabulary into your head, although it will help some. Just gradually speak it more, listen to it more, and study a little bit every day, and I am sure you will do just fine.

Thanks again for buying my book. If you have a minute,

please leave a positive review. You can leave your review by clicking on this link:

Leave your review here. Thank you!

I take reviews seriously and always look at them. This way, you are helping me provide you better content that you will LOVE in the future. A review doesn't have to be long, just one or two sentences and a number of stars you find appropriate (hopefully 5 of course).

Also, if I think your review is useful, I will mark it as "helpful." This will help you become more known on Amazon as a decent reviewer, and will ensure that more authors will contact you with free e-books in the future. This is how we can help each other.

DISCLAIMER: This information is provided "as is." The author, publishers and/or marketers of this information disclaim any loss or liability, either directly or indirectly as a consequence of applying the information presented herein, or in regard to the use and application of said information. No guarantee is given, either expressed or implied, in regard to the merchantability, accuracy, or acceptability of the information. The pages within this e-book have been copyrighted.

Made in the USA
Middletown, DE
19 August 2015